EME

A Journey in

EMERALD SPIRIT

A Journey into the Irish Heart and Soul

DAVID PHILLIP STANG

MERCIER PRESS

MERCIER PRESS
Douglas Village, Cork
www.mercierpress.ie

Trade enquiries to COLUMBA MERCIER DISTRIBUTION,
55a Spruce Avenue, Stillorgan Industrial Park, Blackrock, Dublin

1 85635 410 5

10 9 8 7 6 5 4 3 2 1

Printed in Ireland by Colour Books Ltd

To Sarah Elizabeth Stang

CONTENTS

ACKNOWLEDGEMENTS

I thank my wife, Sarah, for cheering me on and for providing insightful feedback, editorial advice and typing assistance.

I am also indebted to several Irish friends who have taken the time to critique the draft chapters. Each of them has reviewed at least one chapter, and some have reviewed each one: Tomás Breathnach, Denis Casey, John Collins, Frank Duggan, John Fraher, Anne Kenny, Eddie Lenihan, Morgan Llywelyn, Cait Ní Lochlainn, Tom Looney, Danny Moriarty, John Moriarty, Breandán Ó Cíobháin, Denis O'Connor, Steven O'Shea, Ger O'Sullivan, Mickey Ned O'Sullivan, Steve Rowe and Eddie Weij. I am obliged to these friends for the sound advice and information they have provided.

Many also contributed original information used in the book. I am most grateful for this valuable information, which enabled me to provide so many poignant quotations.

I am also appreciative of others who helped. Charlotte Holmes and Jim Brasfield, for encouraging me to write the book; Sonia Schorman, for typing several versions of the manuscript; Eileen Connolly and Michelle O'Brien for their help in typing; my late grandfather, Harry D. Phillips, and my late mother, Louise Phillips Stang, for telling me stories about Ireland when I was too young to speak, but old enough to listen.

Very special thanks to Mary Feehan, Eimear O'Herlihy and Aisling Lyons of Mercier Press for editing the manuscript so adroitly that its readers may more easily discover for themselves much of what I found so uniquely interesting about the Irish.

I am grateful to Beverley Fry for her striking illustrations, and to John Eagle for the use of his magnificent photograph for the cover.

There are others whom I undoubtedly should have thanked by name but, due to a possible oversight, have not mentioned. Without the kind, gracious and generous assistance of so many people – those who I interviewed and quoted, and those who gave me encouragement and suggestions, nearly all of whom are Irish – this book would never have happened.

FIRST CONTACTS WITH THE IRISH

I fell in love with the Irish a long time ago sitting on my maternal grandfather's knee. His father, John Robert Phillips, escaped the Irish famine of the 1840s as an infant sailing with his mother from the port of Baltimore, County Cork in Ireland to the port of Baltimore, Maryland in America. What my grandfather, Harry Dalrymple Phillips, told me about Ireland he had learned from his father who in turn had been educated about Ireland by his own mother. Over a century and a half ago, she had slung her baby boy over her hip as she climbed up the gangway of the sailing vessel which carried them both across the stormy Atlantic.

I learned from my grandfather that Ireland is a country of a thousand shades of green; it rains a lot there, which makes green things grow and glisten; and the people are friendly, kind, believe in fairies and love to laugh.

These were formative and important early lessons about Ireland which implanted deep within my boyish psyche an intense curiosity about Ireland, a place that seemed to me to be a magical fairyland, rather than a sovereign nation full of real people.

It wasn't until a few years after my grandfather's death that I actually got to see Ireland firsthand. I had become a lawyer and

11

was visiting Ireland on a business trip to Bantry Bay in 1971 to learn about Ireland's deep-water port, the only one that then existed in the western hemisphere. I was thinking of my grandfather as I awoke at sunrise to look out the airplane window and see below for the first time Ireland's green fields and grey stone boundary walls. We were beginning our descent for landing. The rosy early sun cast a sheen on the River Shannon and its surrounding rural landscape. It was a poignant moment for me because – under the influence of the sun's glowing dawn rays – the dew-covered fields of Ireland did look like a fairyland.

When I stepped out of the airport, I had a powerful mystical experience. The moment my foot touched Irish soil I felt like I had come home. It was not only as if I had been in Ireland before and therefore the place felt familiar. It was more than that. I felt that I belonged in Ireland and that my thirty-two years in America had been in a foreign country.

Seeking to know and understand the Irish has been one of my greatest adventures over the last thirty years and I often feel that I have most of my work still ahead of me.

Most of what intrigues me about the Irish is how their behaviour, manner of speaking and priorities vary so enormously from what I am accustomed to. Some scholarly American friends attribute this to the contrasting nature of city and country life, asserting that the rural people of Ireland are basically no different to those in America. But I've seen enough of rural Americans to observe that their Irish counterparts are a different breed altogether. The horses, cows and sheep in both countries may look alike but their owners are easily distinguishable.

It could be said that I came to Ireland with an objective frame of mind. I notice what is different and try to comprehend how this has come to pass.

Although I've spent many thousands of hours observing, getting to know, and seeking to understand the people of Ireland, there is a lot I have missed, much that I am still confused about, and a good bit still to learn.

If I had spent my entire life in Ireland, I could not have written such a book, because I would not have noticed the things that I, as an American, have found most interesting about the Irish.

One problematic dimension to writing this book is the paradox of time. Over the past nine thousand years of Irish civilisation, much has changed and much has remained the same. This is also true of the one hundred and fifty years since my great great grandmother left Ireland to seek a new home in America and of the years that I have been coming to Ireland. Often, it seems that what has changed is superficial, compared to what has remained the same.

Capturing a new slice of what it means to be Irish, in each chapter, does not mean that I believe the Irish are merely the sum of these slices. They are more than a combination of their most obvious habits, traits, characteristics, traditions and values. They are more than their origins and family history.

Because they are Irish, much about them remains a mystery hidden in mist. They are neither transparent nor very self-revealing. Each time I return to Ireland I discover another layer of the Emerald Spirit.

STORYTELLING STONES

From my first day ever in Ireland up to the present, as I have
driven along her country roads, I have seen stones everywhere I
look. Some are exposed slabs of rock on the sides of steep mountains. Others are fields full of boulders. I see ragged rocky coast-
lines and rounded stones ground mostly by the action of river or
ocean water rubbing stone against stone. Stones of these types
were here even before the first Mesolithic settlers arrived sometime after the ice age, less than ten thousand years ago. Nature
had arranged these stones.

Then there are stones that were placed in their present location by man. These include the Mesolithic and Neolithic standing
stones, stone circles and megalithic tombs. There are stones in
boundary walls, in forts, castles, dwelling houses and graveyards.
These visible creations, some in place for over five thousand
years, are still standing. Many are still in use and others are ruins.

But why so many ruins? How did the stones become ruins?
More importantly, why do they remain ruins? In one sense, the
ruins are the result of nature, following human abandonment or
neglect. The timber, joined together to support the roofs, to create
doors or provide frames for window panes, rots and collapses,

while the stone withstands weathering. In many cases the abandoned cottages in ruins were occupied by those who died in the famine of the 1840s or left the country to avoid starvation. They remain as symbols of poverty and desolation.

But why are the ruins still standing? Why have they not been cleared, and the land on which they stood returned to pasture, the stones recycled into other buildings or restored or made into monuments or historic treasures? There are several reasons for this. The first is that until very recently, Ireland was a poor country with few financial resources available for funding restoration and preserving monuments. Such undertakings, by Irish standards, would have been viewed as wasteful luxuries.

But what about the hundreds of thousands of roofless, derelict cottages dotting the countryside? Why not recycle those stones and restore the land between the walls to pasture? One reason is that these ruins and semi-ruins are sometimes used to shelter cattle and sheep. Another is who cares whether the building stands or falls? It's just not worth the bother. The Irish aesthetic is not offended by the presence of ruins. This is a good thing. There is no sweeping of ruins under the rug.

But I suspect that a more occult reason lies in what a scholarly friend describes as the monocosmic world view of the Irish. For at the very heart of the Irish soul there is only one universe, and in that universe co-habit man, beast, angels, saints, apostles, fairies, ghosts and demons. There is no duality of spirit and flesh, mind and body, this life and the next. The bodies of the former occupants of the ruined dwelling houses – be they cottages or castles – may have returned to dust, but their spirits may be presumed to remain present, as if residing in the moss-covered walls of each stone ruin. And, if not residing in the stone walls, then they are passing instead through the walls and walking on the same earthen floors and out into the fields as they did when they were incarnate. It is true that some spirits chose to move on to distant realms. But there are many who chose to cruise their old haunts.

Some of the visible stone ruins such as fairy forts – circular enclosures no higher than three or four feet – are believed by some people to be inhabited by fairies. To knock a fairy fort could result in retaliatory injury, maiming or death. Thus, it is wiser to leave fairy forts standing as well.

Now if a tourist, sipping Guinness in a pub, asks an Irishman sitting next to him at the bar if he believes in fairies and ghosts or the sacredness of stones, the tourist will usually receive one of two answers. The first will be a flat denial: 'That's all a load of rubbish. No truth in it at all. My grandfather believed in all that stuff, but 'twas only because he knew no better.'

The second, and more probable, answer would invoke what the Irish term 'winding 'em up'. Winding them up means, in essence, something like winding up a child's mechanical toy so that it dances and sputters all over the floor. The Irish enjoy verbally winding up tourists so their jaws drop in incredulous reaction to what they have just been told. In this case, your Irishman in the pub will resort to fantasy shrouded hyperbole: 'Why of course there're fairies and ghosts and talking stones. Just last night I saw a fairy host walking across the fields behind my house. It was a full moon, you know. That's when the fairies come out in force. You'd better stay away from them or you'll be stone dead in a few hours from their spells. We've plenty of ghosts here too. My great grandmother – dead for forty years now – lives in our house. We hear her slippers moving down the hall toward the kitchen every evening. She sits by the fire all night and leaves in the morning. That's no harm. She won't hurt us. But it's the haunted houses you best avoid. When you hear the keening of the banshee, you know someone close to you will be dead within days.'

'Now what about the talking stones?'

'There's a standing stone you can see from the bridge. It makes predictions about things. One time it said the Kerry footballers would be defeated by Cork. I'm sad to say the talking stone was spot on.'

The Irishman may tell his friends 'You should have seen the look on their faces when I told those tourists about the fairies, and ghosts and the talking stone. I wound 'em up so tight their eyeballs were bulging out of their heads. The feckin' mad tourists believed every word I told 'em. Can you fathom that? Can you imagine anybody dumb enough to believe such a thing?'

If you overheard the Irishman bragging to his friends at the pub about how he just wound up another bunch of tourists, would that confirm that he believed that fairies, ghosts and talking stones are really just a pile of rubbish? The chances are that if he were a farmer, he'd have a ruin of an old house on his land that he'd let his animals use as a shelter. Even if it were standing a few feet from his newer dwelling house, he likely wouldn't knock it down, perhaps for fear of disturbing an immortal spirit. Ask him how often he walks through the town graveyard at night. That would induce a flinch.

Ask him why he hasn't knocked the fairy fort on his land. If you do, he'd likely turn pale. But then he might recover with a bluff: 'I don't believe in fairies at all, but sure, it's doing no harm there as it is.'

The urban Irish have lost a good bit of their monocosmic consciousness, but not all of it. They have been seduced by dualistic sophistication. They have been taught to conclude that only the ignorant believe in the other world – the place where fairies, ghosts and talking stones exist.

But the rural Irishman is caught between the old and the new beliefs. He'll probably profess traditional Irish monocosmic beliefs to be 'pure superstitions' or *piseógs*, but in his heart and soul there is a lingering adherence to these old traditions.

How could the modern day rural Irish believe in such things as stones which utter prophecies? I ask myself is it in the gene pool, the culture, conditioning or a combination of such possible causes? I believe, but cannot prove, that the best answer is a touch of 'all of the above'. I also suspect it is because many personally feel connected to the 'other world' or have family members who have encountered otherworldly creatures.

But can the stones of Ireland really utter prophecies about the future or tell stories about the past?

There is an ancient legend about the stone of Fal which predicted a line of Irish kings. The stone of Fal had been located on the Hill of Tara, County Meath, the seat of the ancient kings of Ireland. The reign of some of Tara's ancient kings had been prophesied by the stone of Fal, according to the legends of the *Tuatha Dé Dannan* (literally translated: the people of the goddess Anna). These were the people of Ireland who were conquered by the invading European Celts, during the middle of the first millennium, BC. One of their kings was Conn of the Hundred Battles.[1]

One morning Conn arose and went to the battlements of the royal fortress of Tara, accompanied by his three druids, Maol, Bloc and Bluicne, and his three poets, Ethain, Corb and Cesarn.

They went there every day to ensure that no hostile fairies or spirits should descend upon Ireland without his knowing about it. Conn's foot trod upon a stone, and the stone shrieked and was heard throughout all of east Meath.

It took the druids fifty-three days to tell Conn: 'Fal is the name of the stone; it came from the island of Fal; it has shrieked under your royal foot, and the number of shrieks is the number of kings of your seed that will succeed you till the end of time.'

Conn and his companions were enveloped in a mist so thick that they could not see where they were. They heard a horseman announce 'I am not a living warrior, but one who has come back from death. My name is Lugh MacCeithlenn, and I am come to tell you the length of your reign, and the name and reign of every king who shall succeed you in Tara.' He then announced each by name.

These legends generally were perpetuated orally by the poets until first written down during the seventh or eighth centuries. The original manuscripts were copied and amended and re-copied and re-amended. Some of these manuscripts survived and are now kept in museums.

If you hypothesise that there were at least four generations in each century and that the legend of Conn and the stone of Fal originated roughly two thousand years ago, give or take a few centuries, then about eighty generations of Irish people have heard or – in recent centuries – read the legend.

Present day Irish people can speculate, or remember with confidence, that their ancestors believed that these legends were true, even if they, themselves, may entertain some doubts.

Something that has been an article of faith for over twenty centuries will not likely evaporate overnight. There are Irish living today who believe that stones can literally talk about the future as well as the past. Some elderly country people actually tell you about conversations they have had with stones, or encounters they have experienced with fairies, ghosts, angels, spirits or any otherworldly inhabitants. There are thousands of rural Irish who, despite many a public denial, still exist comfortably within a monocosmic universe. One good friend of mine, an elderly woman from County Cork, remarked, 'Of course I have the second sight and can see the other world, but I don't like to talk about it for fear the people will think me cuckoo.'

The other world aside, can the stones really tell stories? Viewed from a geological, palaeontological, archaeological or anthropological perspective, the answer could be an incontrovertible yes. That is yes, in the sense that scholars can 'scientifically' infer stories from their examination of what nature or man has done to, or with, the stones in question. Certainly the superabundance of stones in Ireland, whether affected by nature or man, has a long history of stories to tell.[2]

According to archaeological evidence, it was not until about nine thousand years ago that man first settled in Ireland. That was in the Mesolithic period – Middle Stone Age. The people of this period have been classified as hunter-gatherers, without agricultural knowledge. They roamed the land eating vegetables and fruit where they found them, and hunting fish and wild game.

It was not until three thousand years after the first hunter-gatherers arrived in Ireland, that the Neolithic farmers arrived by boat, with their families, cattle and seed. That was about 4000 BC, or six thousand years ago. Within the next two thousand years – until overtaken by the Bronze Age – these Neolithic (New Stone Age) settlers advanced their civilisation to such a degree that many persons living today are astounded at their feats.

By the archaeological evidence available, one can infer that death and afterlife were of such paramount cultural importance in Neolithic Ireland that enormous resources, mainly human and animal labour, were allocated to the creation of megalithic monuments which served as tombs for societal leaders following their deaths. Megalithic is the right word, as the capstone on one portal tomb, also called dolmen, in Browneshill, County Carlow is estimated to weigh one hundred tons.

Over thirteen hundred and fifty megalithic tombs have been discovered in Ireland. There are four types: court tomb, portal dolmen, passage grave and wedge-shaped gallery grave. The most grandiose of these is the passage grave. The best known example is Newgrange, County Meath. As the name implies, a passage or hallway leads from the ground level exterior of a cairn or mound into the centre in which is located a burial chamber. At Newgrange the burial chamber is of a cruciform shape which contains three separate burial sites. The roof of the chamber is corbelled, meaning that successive layers of stones are balanced around the ring of stones underlying them. Each successive ring is projected in closer to the centre so that a single stone caps the hole at the top of the dome. Many stone huts were also built by Neolithic man using the corbelling principle.

At Newgrange each corbelled stone is in fact a boulder weighing possibly twenty tons or more. The diameter of the circular mound of architecturally arranged boulders is nearly 115 yards. The exterior is rimmed with huge standing stones decorated with elaborately carved, swirling designs.

The enormity alone of this 5,000-year-old structure is a testament to Neolithic genius. But its most impressive feature is that above its east facing entrance is a slit in the wall through which, on the morning of the winter solstice, shines a ray of sunlight down the twenty-yard-long passage lined with standing stones. That ray of sunlight strikes and illuminates the principal tomb within the central burial chamber.

Throughout Ireland many of the Neolithic and Bronze Age stone circles were constructed on the alignment principle. When you ponder for a minute the creation of the Newgrange passage tomb, and others like it and the hundreds of still standing stone circles, you can infer that Irish Neolithic man had achieved an enormous amount of engineering and astronomical learning before the ancient Egyptians had built some of their best-known pyramids.

The stones of Ireland have revealed much to us. But there are other stories they tell us. The Neolithic Irish were not only aware of the movements of celestial bodies, they were also aware of the movements of their enemies. So they built forts with walls eighteen feet high, thirteen feet thick and ninety feet in diameter. These are the dimensions of Staigue Fort in County Kerry. Other splendid examples consist of Dún Aenghus in the Aran Islands and Grianan of Aileach, County Donegal. These mighty fortresses were used to protect their families and livestock from enemy attack.

Passageways, called souterrains, were constructed within and under the thick walls which tunnelled underground up to fifty or more yards outside of the fort, opening into a stream bank covered with bushes or into some other hidden place. Providing for an escape from enemies revealed a capacity for creative planning. But even more sophisticated was the design of the souterrain. It narrowed as it extended out from the fort so that the last few yards contained a tunnel so small in dimensions as to require escapers to crawl on their bellies.

The invading enemy was bound to locate the souterrain and chase after those seeking to escape. But when the invader made his way to the end of the tunnel, crawling on his belly, and stuck his head out of the end of the souterrain, a defender would be standing there with a spear or knife to slay him. If another invader tried to push the corpse out and then exit himself, his head would be chopped off as well. So the invaders were forced to drag the corpses back through the tunnel until it widened enough to allow room for manoeuvering. By this time the defenders could well have made a safe escape.

Another thing the stones tell us pertains to where the forts were located. Staigue Fort is located in a canyon-like enclosure near a mountain-top with high sloping inclines. If the attackers tried to climb down the slopes from the mountain-top they would be vulnerable to being killed by the defenders' arrows or spears. The entrance to the fort faces the sea about three miles away, so the defenders would have early warning of any invaders arriving by boats.

Dún Beg, another Neolithic fort, known as a promontory fort, is located on the top of a cliff on the Dingle Peninsula that extends out into and above the sea. The cliff sides are too steep to allow an attack from the sea. The small part of Dún Beg facing landward is protected by high walls and ringed earthen trenches, rendering any invasion a difficult task. It too has a series of souterrains for escape.

By careful examination of Ireland's many thousand samples of stony evidence, you can spot a particular ruin or monument and be able to discover the era of civilisation from which it came. Each era of civilisation in Ireland borrowed from the past and produced innovations of its own.

During Ireland's Bronze Age (2500–500 BC) men continued to build huts out of corbelled stone, the workman was able to cut timber using his bronze axe and also build his houses using wood. He used bronze digging implements and picks to dig mines from which he retrieved copper, tin, silver and gold, among other minerals to be smelted into metals. The same is true of Iron Age man (500 BC–400 AD). During the Bronze and Iron Ages in Ireland smiths fashioned not only weapons and tools, but also elaborate jewellery out of silver and gold and often set with semi-precious stones. These recovered treasures tell us much about the dress, habits and lifestyles of the people who used such ornamentation.

With the Celtic invasion, which generally coincided with the advent of the Iron Age, came other skills. The metal weapons, tools and jewellery of the Celtic invaders were of their unique design, featuring elaborate curvilinear decorations and smaller gem stones set in gold. Some La Tène designs are found in limestone carvings at Turoe, County Galway and Castlestrange, County Roscommon.

By about the fourth century AD a new type of stone evidence began to appear on the Irish landscape: the Ogham stone. These were vertical standing stones carved with notches containing a coded Roman alphabet. This is composed of sets of up to five strokes or notches carved diagonally across, on one or either side the vertical edge of the stone. Ogham stones were used to mark boundaries, as well as graves.

During the fifth century Christianity was brought to Ireland by St Patrick and other evangelising clerics. With Christianity came two other applications of stonework usage. One was the construction of churches (although most of them were made of timber). The other was carved grave stones. A corbelled church, Gallarus Oratory, was constructed on the Dingle Peninsula in the seventh or eighth century. It is shaped like an upside down boat and was constructed without mortar. The church stands in the same condition as when it was built, some thirteen or fourteen hundred years ago.

The sixth century saw flat grave slabs, vertically erected and decorated with a simple cross shape. Next the slabs began to be chiselled into a rude cruciform shape. Then came five centuries of elaborate stone carving, featuring the Celtic cross with a circle around the intersection of the vertical stem with the cross bar. These carved stone masterpieces contained exquisite Celtic designs and eventually included bas-reliefs of stylised animals and scriptural tales. With each century the crosses grew bigger and more elaborate. The great high crosses of Ireland can be found at several of the well-known medieval monasteries of Ireland.

Beginning in the early ninth century, following the onslaught of Viking raids which began in 795, a new stone architectural creation began to appear. These were the round towers. The entrance door was set about twelve feet above ground level and access was up a timber or rope ladder, which was pulled inside and the door secured. This provided safe refuge for the monks, who also used these innovative tubular stone structures as bell towers and storage sites. These round towers are to be found at the great monasteries and other ecclesiastical sites.

Before very many years had passed the Vikings found a way to attack the monks by throwing piles of timber and branches below the high entrance door and igniting them into a blazing fire. The door eventually burned and the chimney effect created, at the very least, a sauna experience for the assembled monks. When the hot ashes cooled, the Vikings entered the round towers and made off with the valuables.

On 1 May 1169 the Normans arrived in Ireland and in less than three years controlled the country. These were Normans, originally from Normandy, whose king, William, in 1066 killed Harold, the Saxon king, at the battle of Hastings in England. Having conquered England, a century later the Normans had Ireland in their grip. The Normans brought with them another stone architectural innovation: a combination fort and house in the form of a castle. These were simple castles, rectangular in shape, and three or four times taller than they are wide. Their simple design is easy to spot. Along with the Normans came changes in ecclesiastical architecture. Prior to the Normans the stone churches had first been of simple design such as Gallarus Oratory. Under Norman influence, the church windows and doorways in Ireland took on a rounded top, known as Romanesque. Cormac's Chapel on the Rock of Cashel is a splendid example of early Romanesque architecture. Carved above the entrance to the chapel is an array of saint and animal faces. With the influx of new monastic orders from the European continent during the late twelfth and thirteenth centuries came a more elaborate style of Gothic architecture.

Also as a result of twelfth-century ecclesiastical reform the centre of power shifted from monasteries to a diocesan structure, which gave rise to the building of cathedrals. With the cathedrals came elaborate stone carvings associated with burial vaults, baptismal fonts and other decorative architectural features. Statues of saints were carved out of stone. Other stone sculpture, including decorative Celtic animal motifs, became a common feature in cathedrals.

As the centuries passed more architectural innovations occurred. Norman castles added round towers at their corners. Early medieval cities built high walls around them. The castles became even more elaborate.

By the mid-fifteenth century the English Tudor influence began to manifest itself, not only politically with Henry VIII acquiring the additional title of king of Ireland, but also with the introduction of Tudor designs. These were far more elaborately crafted than even the most advanced of Norman influenced architecture. Castle design grew more intricate with the passage of time, except during the Cromwellian period (1644–1650) when many of the previously built monasteries, castles and fortresses were breached, sacked and burnt by Cromwell's troops. Later in the seventeenth century the English forts in Ireland were built in a star-shaped form.

Thereafter came the birth of the great public buildings, like the Royal Hospital, Kilmainham, Dublin, built in 1680. During the eighteenth century, Georgian architecture could be seen abounding in the cities and larger towns of Ireland.

Many grandiose manor houses were built by the wealthy English landlords during the eighteenth and nineteenth centuries. Some would be sacked and burned by the IRA in the early twentieth century.

Out of these centuries of masonry creations some common threads emerge. On one hand, there is a continuum of shelter and fortification. On the other hand, there is an equally strong tradition of building monuments for a more spiritual purpose. From stone circles and megalithic tombs, created over five thousand years ago, this tradition had extended to stone churches, starting in the seventh or eighth century, then to cathedrals starting in the twelfth century and continuing to the present day. Gravestones and burial monuments have been treasured in Ireland for several thousand years.

The Irish have been loath to knock down and destroy these exquisite and creative stone constructions, mainly for practical reasons, but in some cases due to an awesome awareness of, and sensitivity to, spiritual powers.

Visitors to Ireland cannot help but discover for themselves the nine thousand year continuous history of civilisation revealed by stones of many colours and shapes. Stones that were pulled from the earth, chiselled, cut or carved into the right shapes in order to make or mark tombs, standing stones, stone walls, houses, stone forts, castles, churches, cathedrals, roads and statues. Stones that were themselves born several hundred million years ago, aeons before man – the stone user – arrived on the scene.

WHY THE IRISH TALK ABOUT THE
WEATHER FIRST

There is one obvious and several more occult reasons why the rural Irish talk first about the weather. At the beginning of nearly every conversation there is at least a passing reference to the weather, but more usually also some sort of an expository discourse. Such a discourse could include a short description of the weather followed by a commentary on the acceptability or lack of acceptability of recent weather conditions and a wish for a change for the better. Now why would such an entrenched custom come to pass?

Let's consider the single most obvious explanation. As my good friend John Collins, recently retired head of the Met Éireann (Irish meteorological service) facility at Cork airport, put it, 'Bad weather is coming ... It's here ... It's just passed and now we are waiting for the next weather system.'

Notice that John avoided the word 'rain'. The Irish have a wonderful way of denying the undesirable. There is a political correctness adhered to in Ireland when discussing the weather: NEVER SAY RAIN. The matter of rain is handled like the emperor's new clothes. The emperor is naked, but it is not permissible to admit or accept the possibility of his nakedness. It's as if the Irish believe each precipitating droplet must be as large as a goose egg before it can legitimately be called rain.

The politically correct solution has been to find acceptable synonyms for rain, which only hint at the reality of water droplets falling out of the sky. So as not to condemn the Irish in any way for their refusal to utter that four-letter word, it is more humane to recognise the ingenious Irish system for distinguishing one form of rain from another. The Irish have produced a nomenclature for sub-species of rain like the Eskimos have done for snow.

One day last summer I was headed out of town to 'collect' – as they say in Ireland – a friend to help me build a stone wall. Standing on a corner of the road leading to the next town was a little old lady, nearly ninety years of age. She was thumbing a lift with her left hand and holding a plastic bag of groceries with her right. She had a woollen scarf on her head and a winter coat on her back. Her stockings hung in loose folds down her scrawny legs. The way she was twitching her gums made me suspect that she was missing a number of teeth.

I stopped right next to where she was standing, leaned across the seat to open the passenger-side door, and asked if she would like a lift. While sober, one normally doesn't offer a lady a ride in Ireland, because 'ride' means something very different from a lift.

She stepped into the car with an almost vacant expression on her face, placed the bag of groceries between her feet, and closed the door.

It had rained for three days straight and the wind had been howling. The lashing rain had stopped at about noon the day before. This particular morning the wind was still, but there was a noticeable continuing dampness in the air, an almost invisible mist. It was neither hot nor cold. The sky was cloudy and overcast with no sign of the sun.

Without any particular inflection in her voice, the old lady stated, ''Tis a soft day.' That was all she said during the seven-mile journey.

For months I replayed it in my mind and asked what was going on in her geriatric consciousness.

In my experiences travelling around the world, I have found the Irish to be the most talkative of all nationalities. But the meat of this old lady's otherwise lean conversational sandwich was the weather.

It took me nearly thirty years to learn that 'soft day' meant damp with barely visible precipitation, still, overcast, and neither hot nor cold, which the Irish term 'mild'. The dampness, temperature and stillness could be felt on the hands and the face. The stillness could also be heard, through the lack of a whistling wind. It could be seen, through motionless leaves on the trees. The overcast sky could be seen, as well. It seemed, too, that changes in barometric pressure might also be sensed. I have yet to learn whether soft days have any particular odour about them.

It should be noted that one adjective, 'fine', when added to 'soft day', changes the meaning somewhat. On a fine soft day there's at least a trace of the sun, and there's a noticeable improvement in the weather from what had likely been several days and nights of nearly continuous rain.

But then again, the word 'rain' is seldom used by the Irish. The Irish have other ways to say it's raining. If the rain is barely perceptible and accompanied by fog, it's a misty day. If there is some precipitation and the sky is covered by so many cloud layers that they appear greyish-black in colour, it's a dirty day or a dark day. If the day is somewhat dirty, the air slightly warmer than usual and rather still, and the potato plants not more than a few days to a few weeks from having sprouted, then it's a blighty day.

The Irish appreciate fine distinctions of speech as well as of weather. Depending upon the region of Ireland you might be visiting, you will note that various other terms are used to describe increasing intensities of rain in combination with other variables of the weather. But generally throughout the country, if the wind is lashing at gale force and rain is stinging the face in horizontal streams, it is usually known as a fierce desperate day.

If there is no rain at all, it's a lovely day. If there is no rain, and the sun is obscured by a thin but omnipresent, cloud layer it's a bright day. If the cloud cover thickens to create a light grey colour, it is referred to as a dull day. If the sun is shining brightly with a clear blue sky, it's a glorious day. Whatever the gradation, if the day – despite intermittent precipitation – is an improvement over the previous day, the Irish will usually say, 'Thank God for the change in the weather', or 'Thank God for small favours'.

Not only do the Irish have several varying kinds of weather, but the weather is in a near constant state of change. Furthermore, such changes rarely occur uniformly throughout the country, in the same county or even in the same town. You can often look out the window on one side of your house and see rain in the field across the road and look out another window on the other side of your house and see the sun shining brightly.

Given the near constancy of change, the imminent inevitability of at least one of several species of Irish precipitation dropping out of the sky, and the likely geographical irregularity of weather patterns, on even the smallest of scales, guarantees that the phantasmagoria of weather in Ireland is certain to capture one's attention. This has been the case since the first settlers arrived nine thousand years ago. Over the centuries Irish people have developed a praiseworthy terminology for each subtle change in the weather.

There are other reasons why Irish conversations begin with a genuflection to the weather. Every infant in Ireland begins to make sense out of words their parents are using and develops – one word at a time – their own functional initial vocabulary.

A friend, who grew up on a farm in County Tipperary, explained to me how, as a little girl, she had heard about the weather from her mother: 'Each morning my mother would walk out the back door towards the shed, carrying an empty wicker basket, and return with the basket filled with turf for the fire. But one morning I noticed that my mother did something else on the way out.

'Having taken two steps out the back door my mother would stop to inspect the grass, then gaze at the sky where the sun comes up. She would look all around the sky, including where the sun sets, and where the sun lies low during the winter months.

'So when my mother returned from the shed that morning with another basketful of turf, I asked, "Mammy, why do you stop every morning and look at the grass and the sky?"

'"I'm just taking notice of what kind of a day it is and what the weather is likely to be. I take a good sniff. I use my eyes and ears as well. I look at the grass to see if it's dry or full of dew. I look at the sky to see if the sun is peeking through the clouds. I look to the west and south to see which way the clouds are blowing and if storm clouds are coming our way. I watch which way the birds are flying. They know more about the weather than yourself. It's their business to know. I listen to the birds and to the wind, as well. Now that I think of it, I even feel the weather on my face, neck an' hands. My skin tells me if it's hot or cold, dry or wet, windy or still, or halfway in between. I've had my nose to the weather since I was your age. My own Mammy taught me and her mother before her, way back to the beginning of time. Just like by answering your questions I'm teaching you about the weather.'''

Weather affects pasturage, crops and livestock. Ireland's people since Neolithic times have been dependant upon agriculture for their very survival. The weather, on one hand, can produce fertile abundance or, on the other, can cause a depletion of a good part of the food supply. The Irish have had a legitimate self-interest in paying close attention to everyday meteorological phenomena. It is no wonder that the Irish have developed a nomenclature capable of discussing each discrete variation of the weather.

Many foreigners wonder why the Irish fixate on the weather. Some eventually figure it out. Others never seem to catch on. In the latter category I would include a German gentleman I know who lives in Ireland and is in his mid-thirties. This is nearly word-for-word what he exclaimed to me one day:

'Ireland is very beautiful. No von can doubt zat. But talking to ze people zere is very boring. All zey are able to talk about is ze vether, cattle, sheep und fishing. Ze Irish make such a big deal out of ze vether. Zey chust beat it to death. Vot is zere to say about ze vether? Not much. But vat ze Irish have to say about ze vether makes no sense at all. Zey say soft but not hard, dirty but not clean. It's raining all ze time, but zey never admit it. Vat zey say has no meaning.

'Zey giff vether forecasts zat are worth nothing. Zey say: To-day zere vill be a chance of showers mixed mit bright spells, mit ze sun possibly shining intermittently, perhaps not, mit variable vinds and a bit mild, but also perhaps cold. Now zat says nothing at all. Ze Irish vether forecasts are zerefore entirely useless.

'But Ireland is a beautiful country und ze people are nice to be vit ven zey are not talking about ze vether, cattle, sheep und fishing.'

My poor distressed friend, let's call him Klaus, just couldn't catch on. As analytically astute, as philosophically agile as Klaus was as a highly educated German gentleman, he read the Irish all wrong. He made several errors of interpretation.

Klaus failed to understand that the weather always outranks in significance cattle, sheep and fishing, and for that matter, nearly any other subject. He also thought the Irish were highly inarticulate when discussing the weather. He simply didn't grasp their unique meteorological vocabulary. His belief that Irish weather forecasts were meaningless was a failure to understand that the weather in Ireland is usually quite capricious and it would be economically unfeasible, if not technologically improbable, to create a separate forecast for each half-acre field in Ireland.

The weather's constantly changing feature demands unflinching attention and it is used as a means of initiating conversation in Ireland because it is a non-invasive, unobtrusive, unobjectionable way to start talking to someone. Moreover, it is also a very subtle means of presenting weather forecasts of one's soul and obtaining a weather forecast of one's conversant's soul.

If, for example, one Irish person greets another with, ''Tis a fine soft day, altogether', what does that really mean? The 'altogether' reinforces the 'fine', implying that the speaker appreciates the weather and is in a generally good mood. What if the person being addressed responds with, 'Fine soft day, you say? It seems to me we're not out of the wetness yet.' We have just been presented with a hint that the respondent is in a pessimistic, if not a black mood.

But the man or woman alleging the fine softness of the day could not irrefutably leap to the conclusion that his or her friend was in a miserable frame of mind. Even if he or she were correct in the initial assessment, in Ireland there would never be a direct suggestion to the respondent that a negative disposition had been detected. That would be rude, crude, invasive and highly unsophisticated.

Rather the conversation would go on to, 'How's things?' If this gentle interrogation yielded any further evidence of pessimistic irritability, the question would never be asked, 'What's bugging you today?' That too would be excessively intrusive. What would more likely follow would be an oblique expression of sympathy, such as 'I know how things like that can happen.'

If it appears, during the discussion about the weather, that the present mood of the conversant is likely to be unswervingly grouchy, the initiator of the conversation will often switch to a lighter, more joyful theme then gently terminate, so that the parting would be assuredly pleasant.

It should never be underestimated what the Irish can do with the weather when it comes to sky watching or soul probing. So don't be fooled as Klaus was. The Irish are anything but boring when they talk about the weather.

As will be discussed at greater length in the chapter on the other world, the Irish skies – I would be willing to bet – have had a lot to do with shaping Irish spirituality. The cloud layer is often quite low and can take the form of mist or fog. The effect is to bring heaven, or the home of the gods, so close to the earth that you can not only see it, but feel it touching your face.

Mist, which has a common root in Old English and Old Norse, then meant darkness or dimness. This is because mist obscures the sun's light, causing darkness or dimness. Light and darkness are more than mere metaphors in the lexicon of ancient world religions. Darkness is associated with obscurity, evil, harm, cruelty, desolation, Satan and the underworld. Light is associated with enlightenment, purification of the soul, the Divine and the place to which we return where we will dwell forever in bliss.

When you reflect a bit on the Irish vernacular lexicon of weather-related terms you might notice that most fall into one of two major categories. One pertains to the ferocity level of precipitation, while the other concerns the degree of light or darkness. In ascending order of lightness the progression proceeds as follows: black, dark, dirty, dull, bright, sunny. The less the cloud cover, the brighter the light; the denser the cloud cover, the darker it gets.

The Irish can seldom get enough light to satisfy themselves and they grumble about days which, while free of rain, nevertheless fit into the dull to black categories. I believe, though cannot prove, that the Irish hunger for light has a spiritual dimension to it. As Ignatius of Loyola phrased it in his *Spiritual Exercises*, one senses consolation when one becomes aware of the presence of God, and desolation when Satan is controlling one's mind-state. Similarly, the Irish tend to feel consolation when the sun is shining and desolation when the daytime sky is dull to dark.

Ireland is a land of darkness and light. Because of the frequently thick cloud cover the nights in Ireland can be so dark that when standing outside alone on a country road or field you literally cannot see your hand in front of your face. This darkness, and that lesser version brought on by sustained misty or foggy daylight, instills in the Irish a certain melancholy or a depressed state of mind. This is eradicated by a bright, sunny day which can induce an almost manic state of bliss. When you cast your eyes towards the horizon and see, streaming through the cloud cover, majestic rays of light, you can only begin to suspect that the Deity, or at least a mighty host of angels, is close at hand. The majestic rays of light are as plentiful as rainbows in Ireland. And everyone knows about the spiritual magic of rainbows.

The other world presses down daily on the people of Ireland. As a result, the Irish monocosmic consciousness is constantly being reinforced by kaleidoscopic skies.

The Irish, with their acute sensitivity to the weather, also recognise climatic wind patterns. They have names for these as well. *An Scairbhín* (pronounced Ahn Skaraveen), for example, means a cold wind from the north which comes in the late spring or early summer after a period of mild, calm weather. Another is *Scairbhín na gCuach* (pronounced Skaraveen na Gooach), the term used in South Kerry to describe a wind that heralds the coming of the cuckoo. These two terms are, more or less, the obverse of the term, 'Indian summer'.

Whenever a chilling wind moves down from the Arctic, it is known as a 'fresh' wind. The word fresh, rather than being associated with vegetables or flowers, is more normally intended to mean cold and chilly. Thus, assume a hearty Irish swimmer invites you into the lake, bay or sea for a swim. Agreeing, you ask, 'How is the water?' The swimmer, more often than not, will answer, 'Nice and fresh'. What this means is that if you stay in the water for as long as five minutes, your skin will turn blue. If you can stand it for up to ten minutes, you have either come down with a case of terminal hypothermia or a total loss of sanity.

Before leaving the subject of the Irish sensitivity to winds blowing from various directions, let's consider one additional example. This pertains to a high-pressure front blowing across Ireland from the dry northern European land mass. It can sometimes last for a few days. The Irish, more accustomed to masses of damp air which blow across the Atlantic, notice how dry the skin feels on their face and hands as a result of this wind. They notice its direction and properly recognise it as a 'dry wind from the east'.

I have often wondered what was going on up in the sky that corresponded with the panoply of subtle descriptions of the weather employed with such precision by the Irish. I decided to ask my Met Éireann friend, John. On the way to Cork I tried to remember everything I could from what I already knew about why there is so much rain in Ireland and about other factors pertaining to its climate. During my time as a naval intelligence officer, I had taken courses in ocean science and had been on a few oceanographic cruises. On one voyage we were doing research in the Gulf Stream, a warm, powerful ocean current which originates off the east coast of Florida, works its way northward up the western Atlantic coast and then turns eastward, crossing the Atlantic and runs right into the south-west coast of Ireland. The warmth of the Gulf Stream is partly responsible for the palm trees that thrive on the south-west coast of Ireland in the dead of winter. I learned how the oceans play such a significant role in the world weather picture. They evaporate, tossing enormous amounts of moisture into the air. By the time the weather reaches Ireland, it is air saturated with moisture.

I learned how the air temperature over islands surrounded by ocean is moderated by the temperature of the adjacent waters. Water temperature changes far more slowly than air temperature. That Ireland is surrounded by water is a major reason why the temperature in Ireland varies less than 10 or 15 degrees Fahrenheit (6–9 degrees Celsius) on an average day. That is why Irish people consider it quite cool in Ireland at 45°F (7°C) and warm at 65°F (18°C). At 70°F (21°C), when the sun is shining brightly, you often see men living in rural areas and in small towns taking off their shirts, hoping to acquire a suntan.

When the air temperature rises to about 80°F (27°C), which it rarely does, some of the old country women say, 'The tongues of the fires of hell are licking away at us. It's a sure sign of the Devil'. There are seldom widespread and sustained hard frosts in the winter, nor a multitude of severe sunburn cases in the summer. On the coldest night of the year in the chilly midlands, which lack the coastal warming influence, the temperature only drops to a low of about 21°F (-6°C). The coldest temperature ever recorded in Ireland was -3°F (-19°C). This occurred on 28 January 1881. The hottest day ever recorded was 92 degrees (33°C) in July 1876.

But the winds do blow hard off the North Atlantic during the Irish winter months with bone-chilling intensity. Despite the comparatively mild temperatures, the wind chill factor can be hard at work.

Ireland is close to the northern European land mass, which sends hot air westward toward it in the summer and cold air in the winter. But the prevailing winds are from the south and south-west, the direction from which the warmth-bringing Gulf Stream is flowing. The Atlantic Ocean chills the air blowing over Ireland in the summer because of the comparatively small degree of fluctuation in water temperature year-round. For the same reason, the Atlantic warms the air blowing over it near sea level in the winter, thus moderating Irish air temperature year-round.

I asked John if the Irish omitting the word 'rain' from their conversation wasn't a blatant denial of ambient reality

"Tis, but it makes one feel better. With all the rain we get in Ireland we need everything we can lay our hands on to make us feel better.'

I began to reflect on this thought about needing all the help we can get to avoid having to face the reality of so much rain.

Two days before it had been raining buckets and the day before that the sun had been shining with uninterrupted brightness. On the day of the downpour I stepped into a butcher shop to buy some meat. The woman behind the counter noticed the rain dripping off my cap and jacket. But did she mention the torrent bouncing off the streets?

No. She was clearly aware of it but she greeted me with the words, "Twas a lovely day altogether, yesterday. Now wasn't it?'

This led me to recognise that the Irish put the best spin on the weather they can. They know that no matter how bad it is, it's not going to last forever. The Irish seem to think about the weather more with their hearts than their intellect.

I began to suspect that this habit may well have influenced the way the Irish put the best spin on nearly every disorder they encounter. It's a brilliant survival strategy. I've encountered numerous examples of the Irish being handed a lemon and then trying to turn it into lemonade. Several years ago the Kerry footballers lost to Cork in the Munster final. The friend with whom I was watching remarked at the end of the game, 'You can't say Kerry didn't put up a brave fight.'

A local fellow I know, who is a mighty man for the drink, wrote off his brand new car by driving it into a stone wall. I heard one of his friends remark, 'At least he's alive to tell about it.'

Another acquaintance was talking about a friend who was terminal with liver cancer. She said, 'Poor Seamus, dying of liver cancer. Thank God it's not brain cancer.'

An ability to see the silver lining in a storm cloud is what enables the Irish to endure several wintry weeks of gale force winds and driving rain, lashing down left and right before suggesting, 'It's fierce desperate weather we've been having just now, but at least we've not been struck by a tidal wave'.

WIT, SLAGGING AND OTHER FORMS
OF
IRISH MENTAL AGILITY

Irish wit is usually associated with humour, but it's really a lot more than humour. Before taking a look at the serious side of wit, let us consider that dimension of wit which induces laughter. 'Slagging', 'codding' and 'winding a person up' are three forms of Irish wit. Slagging means ridiculing a person, usually a friend, by exaggerated references to his or her inadequacies. Codding is a milder form of teasing. Winding a person up means fabricating or exaggerating a story to fool the listener.

Without allowing the topic of Irish weather to fade too far in the distance, let us examine a hybrid of codding and slagging intended to 'wind-up' a distraught German tourist.

The Germans have a reputation – whether or not deserved – for lacking humour and for taking everything literally. Last summer, Brendan, a friend of mine, was sitting in a pub sipping a pint of Guinness when four German motorcyclists walked in and sat down next to him at the bar. They were dressed in black leather jackets, pants, gloves and boots, and had parked their bikes outside the pub. Having ordered a beer the one sitting next to Brendan asked him, 'I vonder if you could help me vit a question about ze vether. My three friends and me, have been here for ten days on holidays and it has rained every day. The sky has been black or dark grey and the sun has not shined vonce. All it has done is rain day and night. Could I ask you vat is going on?'

'Well now, wouldn't you know, you're right in the middle of monsoon season,' Brendan responded.

'You mean ze Irish really have monsoons here?'

'Why of course we do. Monsoon is an ancient Irish word that the rest of the world has copied from us.'

'Zen how long does your monsoon season last?'

Brendan, seeing that he had the German visitor nearly wound up tight as a top, declared, 'Seldom longer than say, ten or eleven months at a time and here you are in the dead centre of it.'

The German gulped down the last few ounces of his beer, slammed down the glass against the bar and declared, 'Ze people in ze travel agency in Chermany never told us zat. Ven I get back, I am going to give zem the Devil about zis. Ze very idea of zem sending us here in the middle of monsoon season.'

Brendan told me that the German then told his three friends what he'd just heard and they looked so depressed they each ordered another round and whisky chasers to go with it, seeking relief from their misery.

A neighbour's son, who was twelve years old at the time, said that he liked to slag the American visitors who get off the big tour buses and run into gift shops. He said they often ask him about leprechauns. Are they real? Has he seen one? He tells me that he always answers in the affirmative, saying he sees them all the time. They stay in his mother's flower garden at night and usually wear green hats and smoke long-stemmed clay pipes.

Winding up Yanks is great sport at some pubs. American golfers would drive down to a pub to take in a slice of local colour. The pub in question is also a general store, butcher shop and a petrol station offering minor repairs. Its raftered ceiling is filled with nearly two hundred years of dust and cobwebs. The floor is covered with sawdust. The visiting golfers are often advised by their friends who have been there before to go sit at the bar, order a drink, then watch what goes on. The proprietor, unbeknown to his American visitors, likes to put on a little show intended to wind them up so tight their eyes would bulge.

At one end of the bar is the butcher shop with a large slab of bacon resting on a butcher block. In the warmer summer months as many as two dozen flies could be tracking around the top and sides of the big chunk of bacon.

Often a customer would pull in to have his tank filled, then step inside to buy some bacon while paying for the petrol. The proprietor would come in from the fuel pump, snatch the fly-covered slab of bacon with his black greasy hands and cut off a few slices with his butcher knife. He'd act disgusted at the sight of the flies, take off his greasy tweed cap and slap it down hard on the bacon slab, often killing a dozen flies with one blow. Then he'd put his cap back on his head, flick off each dead fly sticking to the slab of bacon with a separate snap of his fingers. As the Americans look on in horror, the proprietor would smile at them and say, 'You know I'm a real hoor for the hygiene'.

Slagging and winding up are the roughest form of Irish wit and are indeed pervasive. But they represent only a fraction of that aspect of Irish wit which is linked to the humorous. A milder form of this type of humour is represented by the jokes the English love to tell about the Irish, the central theme of which is the thick Paddy. The adjective 'thick', as used in this context in England and Ireland, means a stupid person. The Irish like to retell the English jokes about 'Paddys' as Kerryman jokes, as the Kerryman has an undeserved reputation for lacking cognitive capacity.

There are more Irish jokes in circulation than the 'Paddy' or 'Kerryman' jokes. Irish jokes, to my way of thinking, are funny because of the laughter-inducing, unpredictable, ingenious, if not bizarre, twists contained in the punchline.

Although I've heard many dozens of examples over my thirty-plus years exposure to Irish jokes, I've limited myself here to a few treasures which I hope may be as titillating to you as they have been to me.

There's the one about Kathleen and Michael who grow up as children on adjacent farms. By the time they were sixteen they had begun dating. This relationship continued over the years.

Kathleen rang up Michael to invite him to dinner for the

twentieth anniversary of their first date. She pulled out the linen tablecloth, crystal goblets, candlesticks, and other best ware and set a proper table.

Michael arrived, ate his dinner and never said a word. This dismayed Kathleen somewhat so she turned to Michael, asking him, 'Michael, haven't you noticed the linen tablecloth, crystal goblets, candlesticks and the lot? Don't you think it's about time we started thinking about getting married?'

'Not a bad idea at all, Kathleen, but at our age, who would have us?'

There's a certain sadness in this joke, but also a verbal twist that brings a smile. The Irish have had centuries of sadness, and their ability to see the humorous side of their calamities has served them well.

Another one concerns a priest who arrived at his new parish on a day there was a funeral at which he was required to officiate. After the sermon he mentioned it was his custom to say a few kind words about the deceased, a eulogy of sorts. But since he never met the deceased and barely had time to shake hands with the family, he was unable to present the eulogy himself. So he asked that several parishioners stand up, one at a time and express some fond memories of the dead man.

No one budged. Not a sound. 'That's not a very Christian response,' said the priest, 'I'm not asking for everyone to speak. Only one or two would do. The poor man is dead. There will be no absolution, no communion, no dismissal until at least one of you stands up and says a few kind words about the deceased.'

There was again an initial silence. Then slowly an elderly man in the back pew stood up, crossed his arms, and said, 'His brother was worse'.

No nation is more artful than the Irish when it comes to detecting and reporting subtle contrasts.

It seems as if we've gone from marriages to funerals without mentioning any of the good stuff that happens in between. The Irish seldom use the word 'naughty'. They prefer the adjective 'bold', which means the same thing, but with a little more energy behind it. At the risk of being bold, I'll dare to broach the subject pertaining to the human reproductive process, which no heaven-desiring Irishman would ever do in the presence of a priest.

The next story concerns an Irish golfer, of whom there are hundreds of thousands. This particular golfer had a stroke of bad luck on the course, so he got up at the crack of dawn and went out to the golf links to practise. He still couldn't get it right. The golfer cursed to himself, 'I can't hit this miserable ball worth a damn'. Suddenly a leprechaun appeared and asked the golfer what seemed to be the problem. The golfer said, 'I can't drive the ball, chip it, or putt it. I make a complete bollix of the whole lot'.

Reaching into his pocket, the leprechaun pulled out a crystal vial which he handed to the golfer, saying, 'Drink that down real quick. It'll improve your golf game and, for that matter, your sex life as well'. The golfer drank the magic potion and handed the empty vial back to the leprechaun – who suddenly disappeared.

Immediately his golf game improved to near perfection. His sex life, which had been almost non-existent for years, began to blossom as well. A year went by and the golfer thought he should return to the same golf course where he had met the leprechaun and thank him for 365 days of near total rapture.

When the leprechaun appeared the man said, 'I wanted to thank you for a splendid year. The golf couldn't have been better and the sex was good.'

'Not so fast, my man, I want a complete report. I want details. Let's start with the golf.'

'All right,' said the golfer, 'I won every match I played. I set new records for every course I played. I hit more holes in one than anyone else in the history of the sport. I'm the world champion, named number one, and my picture is on the front page of every sporting magazine there is.'

'Good. That's better. That's what I want to hear. Now to the sex.'

The golfer thrust out his chest with pride and proclaimed that he had slept with four women in the last year.

'Four women? Only four? You call that an achievement?' asked the leprechaun.

'I do indeed,' said the golfer, 'considering the fact that I'm the local parish priest.'

The ironic and unpredictable twist which catches you off guard is one good reason why Irish humour is truly an art form.

While we're on the subject of priests and sex, we'll move into our next tale.

Often Irish priests spend a few years working in England, Canada or America, among other places. This particular Irish priest was in Manhattan hearing confessions one afternoon. A man came into the confession booth and said, 'Father, my name is Solomon Goldblatt, I'm ninety-six years old and I'm having sex twice a day with a good looking twenty-five-year-old woman.'

The unimpressed priest barked out, 'You say your name is Solomon Goldblatt? You must be Jewish?'

'I am, Father.'

'If you're Jewish, why in God's name are you in here telling *me* all this?'

'Father, I'm telling everyone.'

The word wit is usually, these days, associated with the kind of humour that can generate an explosion of laughter. But its initial usage in the English language pertained to our mental faculty or the seat of our consciousness. This evolved into the faculty of thinking and reasoning, thus understanding and intellect. To be half-witted was to lack such faculties. To be at one's wit's end meant that one's mind had been stretched to its limit and therefore the person remained perplexed and at a loss in fathoming a problem. The 'five wits' was a term used to refer to our five senses. To have our wits about us was to be sensibly aware and mentally astute. Wit also meant one's intellectual powers, and the conscious capacity for critical thinking. 'Out of one's wit' meant out of one's mind, or insane. The Anglo-Saxon root of the word is *witan,* which means 'to know'.

Wit also meant a practical cleverness, ingenuity or skill. To have the wit to train a horse, for example, meant the wisdom, experience and good judgment necessary to accomplish the task effortlessly.

Taken a step further, it also came to be used to connote an ability to make apt associations of thought, or invent innovative analogies, which have the effect of surprise and delight due to their quickness of expression and their unexpectedness. A person with great wit, therefore, was respected as much for his genius, talent and intellect as much as he was for his quick and entertaining delivery. A man of wit was also a man of experience, knowledge, discernment and judgment, but also quite practical, with the capacity for lightning quick comprehension of nearly any idea or thought.

It might be entertaining to note that traditionally under the Common Law, testamentary capacity required the testator to possess a full-witted awareness of his possessions and precisely how he intended to dispose of them. An exception to this rule developed over time. It permitted a testator to be mad as a hatter, so long as he had occasional lucid intervals. If his will were written and executed during one of these lucid intervals, however infrequent they might be, he would be determined to have possessed testamentary capacity.

Having considered 'wit's' etymology, we can better apply that sense of the term to what is witty about the Irish mind. What occurs to me as I reflect on Irish wit is its unique ability to grasp the essence of an issue and describe it with an incisive discernment, yet also be able to describe the perception in a way that entertains and amuses. This includes observing minor disasters and seeing within them something that induces healing laughter rather than a victimhooded self-pity.

Danny Moriarty, known around town as Danny the Breadman, told me one day about a man who moved into the area only to be plagued by his next-door neighbour who blackguarded him so often with such intensity that the poor man rarely spent a day in which his neighbour had not caused him some new kind of trouble. Members of the community felt great sympathy for the poor man and would ask him what he thought of his awful neighbour. In a cheery voice the man would answer, 'I don't have an unkind word to say about that man, but what the whole town is saying about him must be true.'

Danny is a quick-witted man himself. Not long ago I encountered him in the local cemetery overseeing the paving of its paths. At the time I was showing some visitors from America the holy well located there. Not missing a chance for some gentle slagging, Danny commented, 'I'm afraid you're too late to purchase a plot here. They're all taken.'

'Well, what about renting me some space for just a few years.'

Danny smiled and delivered me a poignant one liner, 'Ashes only'.

Five years ago, I was having tea with a couple of Irish stonemasons and some other tradesmen who were working with me on a house construction project. It happened to be the day the local town was having its fair. The fair is always held in August, and even though it was the biggest market day of the year, where farmers for miles around brought their cattle and sheep to town to sell to the out of town buyers, it has a touch of the Lughnasa spirit. On fair day the pubs in town do great business and, by the end of the day, sobriety is usually not to be found for miles around.

Nearly everyone takes the day off to celebrate. Thus, the masons were breaking with tradition and making a big sacrifice not to join in the fair day festivities. Instead they lapsed into a few moments of nostalgia. They remembered what fair days were like long ago, when they were much younger, and began telling stories. I recognised that what they said exemplified Irish wit in a double sense. First, their expressions were full of wit, in the humorous sense. Secondly, much of what they described entailed others' quick-wittedness:

In fair days gone by things were different. The farmers used to bring their sheep up to the old church in Killowen and keep them there for the night before marching them into the town the next day. The farmers would take turns standing watch over the sheep during the night.

A local publican was the first man to use pens to hold the sheep. Before that they'd run everywhere. The farmers would go into the pubs where the buyers would stand them drinks. It was the decent thing for a buyer to do, but it would take a lot of beer before you'd get a Kerry farmer drunk enough to sell his sheep cheaply. Then the deal would be made by spitting on one's palms, rubbing them together, then touching hands, like shaking hands, but instead just touching. When the farmer would be in the pub he'd have his helper mind the sheep. But often the helper would leave the sheep to go get a drink for himself, and the sheep would run all over, shitting on anything in sight.

One time old Dr Quinlan looked out his surgery window and saw the sheep shitting all over his door step. So he told the helper to keep his sheep away from the surgery as he had patients coming in all day. The helper was drunk and told him to 'shag off'. So Dr Quinlan stepped outside and hit your man a wallop the likes of which had never been seen before, and your man went down like he was stone dead, his face buried in sheep shit. Then Dr Quinlan dragged him inside, sewed three stitches in your man's head, and tossed him out the door again. Dr Quinlan was always a gentle fellow and a kindly person. He'd tip his hat; he was a real gentleman.

There was another episode during a sheep fair around September. That's the time when the rams are mating with the ewes, and the rams get jealous of each other and start fighting because each ram wants all the ewes to himself. A farmer brought a couple of rams to the fair hoping to sell them for breeding, and one got away and went walking down the street past Moriarty's Garage where he saw his own face in the plate glass window that ran from floor to ceiling in the front of the garage. He thought it was another ram, so he charged the window with a mighty force, went right through the glass and cut himself 'fierce bad', so there was blood all over the floor and all the new cars on display.

One fair day a sheep farmer from Sneem tried to be a little too cute for his own good. He went to Jack, the barber, for a haircut. Now your man from Sneem was nearly completely bald. He had only a scraggy fringe hanging down over the top of his ears and around the back of his head. When Jack had finished, your man asked what he owed for the haircut. Jack said 'Two pounds fifty.' Your Sneem man said, 'Jaysus Christ Almighty, I have hardly a hair left on my head and you're charging me the full price?' Jack shouted back at your man, 'I only charged you a pound for the haircut, and another one pound fifty for trying to find your fecking hair.'

Although Ireland is honoured as the land of saints and scholars and although famous Irish scholars are generally revered by the common man, there is another kind of person who is also highly respected in Ireland. He is known as the self-taught man.

How is this related to wit? A sharp intellect is an integral dimension of wit. Many people tend to associate intelligence with education. There is a common belief, not always well founded, that dropouts are stupid and PhDs are very intelligent. This is in part because many educational systems are designed to select the best and the brightest and move these bright students forward. As a result, the brightest tend to end up being well educated and the less academic left to a future in the unskilled labour market.

Until recently in Ireland only the students with the best exam results could get into university. However those with the best results and those who are the brightest are not necessarily the same. There are numerous very bright people in Ireland who, educationally, never formally progressed beyond their primary or secondary education. One finishes primary school at age twelve, while eighteen is the age of secondary school graduates.

There are a number of other reasons why there are so many bright Irish people walking around with only primary or secondary education. One has been the lack of places in universities. Also, the cost of going to university can be very expensive. In addition a large number of Irish primary and secondary students, although quite bright, simply hate school. Another reason is that many still follow their fathers and learn their trades instead of going on to university.

Even though more family or societal pressure in Ireland to obtain a university education has developed, there are many older people who had the brain power to go to university, but either lacked the desire, or, due to economic circumstances, their services were needed to help support the family.

One of them we'll call Fergus. He was forced to drop out of primary school to help support his family. He is illiterate in the sense that he can't read or write. Yet, Fergus is very much a genius. He has a burning curiosity about what is going on around him and, as a result of that curiosity, he became a self-taught man. He taught himself nearly all of the building trades, hence he can do carpentry, masonry, plumbing, roofing, electrical work, plastering and painting. Additionally, Fergus loves traditional Irish dancing and is expert at it. He has a well deserved reputation as a great hunter and fisherman. He has won major fishing contests and he taught himself to tie flies.

When Fergus catches a fish, he cuts open the fish's guts and discovers what the fish has been eating. If he doesn't recognise the type of bug the fish has swallowed, or he doesn't already have a fly in his tackle box patterned after it, he'll lift the bug out of the fish's stomach, dry it out, take it home and, by sheer creativity, make one from scratch, using feathers, silk thread and other materials, that ends up looking like a perfect replica.

I asked Fergus how he wins so many fishing contests.

'I've learned to think like a fish. In the hottest days of summer when there's been no rain for days, the fish become sluggish and stay down at the bottom of the lake, where it's cooler. When the rain comes down hard, it releases a lot of muck into the streams and bags of worms along with it. This washes down into the lake and makes it muddy. When it's muddy and you are a fish, you know there's a good dinner of bugs and worms to be had. So on those hot, dry summer days when the fish are sluggish, I'll go to a stream feeding into the lake and kick a rake of earth into the water. When the muddy water reaches the lake and the fish see and smell it, they go mad for a big dinner. That's when I cast my fly.'

Fergus uses a similar kind of ingenuity in solving problems related to building construction by building ramps, improvising special scaffolding, and a host of other innovations. He's as quick-witted as he can be.

Dan Sullivan-Christian, is a mechanical genius who can take apart a machine, never having seen one like it before, and find the broken piece, then craft out of metal a clone of the needed part and reassemble and render the machinery fully operable within a matter of hours. He was never educated as an engineer, nor was he ever a university student. He just has a hungry curiosity about all things mechanical and how to fix them. People for miles around bring their malfunctioning equipment to his door to be fixed.

Batty Batt O'Sullivan, God rest his soul, died a few years ago in his early eighties. The bell tower chimes in the Dawros church in County Kerry were dedicated in his honour. They chime the Angelus every day at noon and at 6 p.m.

Batty was a storyteller or *seanchaí* (pronounced shan'ah'kee), sailor, farmer, geographer, historian, current events specialist and publican. He had sailed to nearly every port in the world while in the Irish navy and US and British merchant marine. He was known as Batty the Sailor. He knew the history of nearly every nation in the world, at least, of those he had visited. He listened to international radio for news broadcasts, read the *Irish Times* every day and subscribed to the *Economist* and other news magazines. He read so many hours a day that by middle age he was wearing, out of necessity, Coke-bottle-lensed reading glasses.

Batty was a walking encyclopedia. He was the only person I have ever met who could hold my attention for hours at a time. He had studied on his own, and mastered the ancient Irish art of storytelling. He could create suspense so thick you'd nearly bite your fingernails. Donncha Ó Dulaing, whose radio program featured Ireland's leading *seanchaí*, had interviewed Batty. The day the interview was broadcast Batty sat by his radio listening to himself talk. The next day he died of a heart attack.

At least two other Irish friends of mine are similarly competent in a multitude of undertakings. Peter Enright, a plumber from Drumcollogher in County Limerick, effortlessly commits to memory the entire plumbing system of each job he has worked on, so that when a customer rings to discuss a problem, Peter can usually give an accurate appraisal over the phone. He taught himself welding, physics, chemistry, metallurgy and the properties of each heating fuel. He also taught himself to play the guitar and performs in a band every weekend.

Damien de Barra, originally from Waterford, is another self-taught man. His profession is jewellery making, and his stunning designs are well-known all over the country. Damien is also a sculptor, painter, falconer, yacht builder, sailor, musician and horseman. He learned all these skills by carefully watching how others practised their trade. Such omnicompetence is quite common in Ireland.

Danny the Breadman was born in Kenmare two days before Christmas 1940. His father was a labourer who died at age forty-two when Danny, the youngest of seven children, was only a year old and his oldest sibling was thirteen. Under the circumstances it was a near miracle that their widowed mother was able to keep the family fed and clothed. They each finished primary school and entered the work force.

Danny joined up with two brothers, Mike and Johnny, who had taken over a small bakery from a retired couple. The two brothers baked while Danny delivered.

In 1975 Danny's curiosity drove him into becoming an expert in local history. The impetus that launched Danny's avocation as local historian came in the form of the Lawrence Collection of photographs of Kenmare taken by Robert French at the end of the nineteenth century.

One of the photographs shows a horse-drawn day car parked outside the Lansdowne Arms Hotel, at the corner of Main and Shelbourne streets in Kenmare, while the visiting tourists were inside having tea. The teams of horses pulling such cars would start out in Bantry, County Cork, and stop at Glengarriff and Kenmare on the way to Killarney, County Kerry. Others began in Killarney and ended up in Bantry. Danny's curiosity led him to discover how the touring company kept stables in each of these towns, from which a team of fresh horses would be taken and hitched up to the car while the tourists were having tea.

Danny felt drawn to do some more detective work about the history of Kenmare. He went to the Kenmare library, which had been funded originally by Andrew Carnegie, and found a book by the Sixth Marquis of Lansdowne on the ownership of lands in the general Kenmare area, from the Cromwellian period in the mid-seventeenth century up to the early twentieth century.[3] The Lansdownes, including the Sixth Marquis, were landlords.

In Ireland, from the Norman conquest in the late twelfth century, until 1920 when Ireland won its independence from England, the term 'landlord' has been closely associated with persons to whom the English king had granted very large estates in Ireland. In this context, the term landlord meant 'lord' of acres of forests and farmlands.

There are many horror stories in Irish history associated with absentee landlords living in England, whose hired land agents in Ireland ruthlessly evicted Irish tenant farmers from the land they worked. Many affected families could find no other available lands and they simply starved to death.

Danny Moriarty soon acquired a reputation for scholarly authority and encyclopedic knowledge. He became a specialist in genealogy. He mastered many original source materials, such as *Griffith's Primary Valuation of Tenaments* (regarding a tax levied in 1850 to support inmates of the local workhouse); the Tithe Allotment Book;[4] *Slater's Trade Directory of 1846*; parish records of marriages, births, deaths; inscriptions from gravestones in all local cemeteries; and the minute books of weekly meeting of Poor Law guardians of the local poorhouse. Danny acquired much data on several thousand people who were associated with Kenmare over the past two centuries to piece together a detailed, working history of the lands and people of Kenmare.

About five years ago, not long after Kenmare established its own website, an Australian woman sent an e-mail indicating that she believed one of her ancestors sailed to Australia from Kenmare in 1849. She asked if there was any information about her ancestor. On receipt of this request Danny went straight to the poorhouse minute book and sent the Australian woman the entry which listed the twenty-five Kenmare poorhouse girls, aged between 14 and 16, who were sent to Australia in 1849 via Plymouth, England. Danny's response was so filled with detail that it included what had been purchased for each girl and how each was outfitted for her journey. Mary Connor was one of the girls on the list, and she was the Australian woman's ancestor. Not long after arriving in Australia, Mary married a British convict who had been sent to Australia for horse stealing.

Danny said, 'My greatest satisfaction in doing this genealogical research is being able to help people from all over the world with Kenmarian roots learn more about their local ancestors'. He achieved his genealogical expertise as a self-taught man.

Eamon Ansbro lives near the town of Boyle, County Roscommon. He hated school, but loved learning. When Eamon was eight years old a friend of his father gave him a book entitled *The Boy's Book of Space*.

By the time Eamon was eleven his new neighbour, a retired aeronautical engineer, was explaining to this wide-eyed boy the names of constellations, what a nebula was, what constitutes a galaxy and how to locate them. Night after night they studied the sky together, peering through a pair of binoculars. While still a teenager Eamon was building his own telescopes and improving their resolution and magnification. He became the first in his secondary school class to complete a course in astronomy.

An astronomer friend of Eamon's encouraged him to go on to university with a view to eventually earning a PhD. That was too time consuming so he did a short course in meteorology. He also acquired a solid understanding of atmospheric physics.

But the pull of the stars and a gnawing curiosity of extraterrestrial intelligence yanked Eamon out of a short-lived meteorological career back into building telescopes. Having built 300 telescopes in his workshop (one of which was an eighteen-inch telescope, which for some years was the largest in Ireland), he founded an optical company in Dublin and manufactured advanced optical systems for export to foreign countries. During all this time he intensified his scientific research into various sub-fields of astronomy. Before he was thirty years old he had discovered a hydrogen envelope around the rings of Saturn, moonquakes and a new star. He has published over sixty letters, articles and papers about astronomy and space.

I asked him what level of formal education he had. Eamon responded, 'Secondary school only, I'm a self-taught man'. When I last visited him, he was building an eighteen-inch and a twenty -six-inch computer-driven telescope so he can study the night sky while sleeping and check his computer the next morning for any new discoveries.

Most of these mentors of mine remain anonymous. Their brilliance has not been discovered other than locally. They have not exhibited themselves on nationwide public display as self-taught men.

But when such a person becomes a writer and his or her books become read by millions and are translated into foreign languages there is no escaping fame. Such an achievement is not easy for a self-taught man. His competition comes from many with university degrees: those who had the privilege of sitting at the feet of renowned poets and novelists in order to learn their craft. But for a self-taught man to become a household name among both common people and the highly literate is an achievement indeed.

The late John B. Keane was such a man, and in recognition of his towering talent, two Honorary Doctorates were conferred upon him. In his hometown of Listowel, John B. Keane was often referred to as Dr Keane, or by his closer friends as John B. Every writer I know has a positive desire to become a fly on the wall who can listen in on intriguing conversations. As a publican and writer John B. Keane daily had that opportunity sitting right across the bar.

These self-taught people were born with a special gift. At the root of their abilities, is an untiring desire to know the how and why about nearly everything and every person they meet. Their curiosity and resourcefulness propel them into erudition.

I found myself compelled to wonder if they were not blessed by missing out on all those additional years of formal education. Would their intense desire to know the how and why of things and their overall curiosity and resourcefulness in finding answers have been enabled or disenabled by years of formal education? Is it possible that their intellectual achievements and knowledge base are richer, more original and more innovative than that of more formally educated people?

Irish wit, as exemplified in the self-taught person, in the etymological sense of the term wit, pertains to an astute ability to recognise and comprehend. It would be difficult to find an example more illustrative of this aspect of Irish wit than their sensitivity to, appreciation for and understanding of, nature. I have met no one in Ireland with a more finely developed awareness of nature and her many intricate processes than my friend Denis.

THE FENCE POST THAT GREW BACK INTO A TREE

About ten years ago in mid-August, Denis Casey asked me if I had seen any signs of deer on my land. I told him that I hadn't seen any deer at all, not one.

This was a few years after my wife, Sarah, and I had bought a small farm in Ireland which we only visited for three weeks at a time, twice a year: in August and December. Nature was something I knew nothing about and cared little about. An exception, of course, was peering at Ireland's serene landscapes and feeling the tranquillity.

I had pretty much cut myself off from the reality of nature. A paradox here is that Sarah has been tuned into nature since birth. As a small child, her friends were lizards, snakes, birds, rabbits and a Shetland pony named Brownie. She spent large portions of her earlier life living in the country, many of those years as an organic farmer. But little of her comprehension of nature seemed to penetrate my own consciousness.

As a workaholic attorney waging legal and political battles in my nation's capital, about the most I had allowed myself was to notice that the city parks contained trees with a few indistinguishable species of birds flying around them, and that dozens of pigeons were usually walking around near park benches looking for scraps of food.

The other exception was trying to get the grass to grow in my garden in Washington. By mid-April the grass had become a rich, thick, bright, bluish-green rug that felt good to walk on. But by July a huge oak had – for at least two months – been shading the garden with its umbrella of leaves. The sun had heated the air to a daily average temperature of about ninety degrees, and the grass had gone nearly bald. An agronomist friend recommended fertiliser, then lime, then shady grass seed and daily watering. None of these worked, so we threw up our hands. I must have concluded that grass going bald was a natural mystery not worth any further pursuit.

It took me till my hair turned white to discover why, since childhood, I had so little interest in nature and therefore so little knowledge of it. My mind was occupied by only those people and events which either facilitated or deterred the realisation of my goals. This was not the kind of mind which easily attuned itself to the signs of nature. The natural world had little direct bearing on either the success or failure of my goals. I never came to discern this particular feature of my mindset until after a dozen years of tutoring on signs of nature by Denis Casey.

As I write these words I hear Denis' question again: 'Have you seen any signs of deer?' I suddenly become aware that he never asked me directly if I had actually seen deer. It was *signs* of deer he was asking about. During our break that day from restoring the cottage and planting shrubs, Denis suggested that we walk the land.

When we had worked our way down to the wooded area near the shore line, Denis asked again, 'Are you sure you've seen no signs of deer? Do you see the patch of grass lying flat over there? That's where they slept last night, I'd say.' Then Denis said, 'Look ahead of you about ten yards in the direction of the stone wall. Do you see the deer droppings on the ground?'

Then he walked me closer toward the stone boundary wall separating our land from that of our neighbour. 'Do you see any other signs of deer?' Denis asked patiently, apparently realising he was dealing with a Yank city boy, who knew nothing of the fundamentals of nature in Ireland.

Denis pointed to a twig extending from a branch overlying the boundary wall. He aimed his fingertips at a small nick on the twig and remarked that one of the deer's front hooves had clipped the twig as it jumped over the wall. He then pointed to a deer's hoof print in the damp earth three feet inside the wall. 'Here's where the craythur landed when he nicked the twig on his way over the wall.'

Lawyering is a highly competitive enterprise and lawyers usually can't stand to be bested. It means only one thing: losing. And that's not acceptable, ever.

There I was, bested by a new friend, a Kerryman whose total schooling was less than half of mine, but whose knowledge of nature so overwhelmed mine that I couldn't possibly compete. As we walked back toward the cottage to resume our afternoon's work, I imagined Denis talking about me to his friends in town: 'Poor craythur. They say he's a successful solicitor over in America. But I can't understand how. The fact that he's survived this long can only be attributed to some kind of a truly supernatural miracle.'

My late mother tried persistently, but futilely, to educate me about nature. For her dedicated efforts she must surely now be receiving her reward in Heaven. As the eldest of three children, I was graced with responsibility for the strong-back chores around the house, like carrying out the rubbish bins, cutting grass, raking leaves, and – my least favourite – pulling weeds. One of my mother's failures was seeking to indoctrinate me, when I was about ten years old, into the difference between flowers and weeds. I pulled out all of the weeds, but also apparently most of the flowers. I was pleased when she quickly gave up and decided that for the sake of preserving the flowers, she had better take over all weeding responsibilities herself.

She didn't do much better on birds. In her mind, there were good birds like robins who eat worms, and bad ones like blue jays who raid other birds' nests, stealing the eggs to break and eat. That's about as much as I remember about good birds and bad birds. She would tap a coin on the plate glass window and shout, 'Get away from here, you nasty blue jay!' I would tell her that the bird couldn't hear her through the window and, even if it could, it wouldn't understand what she was saying. 'They know what I'm saying to them,' she would stress in an effort to convince me. Other times she would look out the large picture window and notice a bird on an inadvertent *kamikaze* mission, about to crash into the glass. 'Birdie, birdie, birdie,' she would exclaim. My mother would hurry out to the flower bed under the window to ascertain whether the bird survived, or if a burial was in order. Mother loved her birds and had feeders all over the garden which she would fill and refill, only to find the squirrels regularly stealing most of their contents.

She also loved her plants and was president of the Ladies' Garden Club. 'Your mother has a real green thumb', her club member pals would remark. But her nature-sensitive aptitude must not have made its way into my gene pool.

All the same, there is something poetic about nature, or at least a good number of poets must have thought so, considering the volumes of nature poetry written over the centuries. Some time during my early teens, I was assigned to read in school a poem that the teacher explained was the first poem ever written in English, and which survived to the present:

Summer is a comin' in,
Lhude sing cuckoo ...

I don't remember if, when I first read the poem, I caught on to the fact that the poet had recognised the seasonal signs; that he regarded loud singing of the cuckoo and his other examples as indicators of the imminence of summer.

Being a city boy, it was easier for me to grasp Ezra Pound's signs of winter, which he intended as a parody of the Old English poem about summer. It was about 'winter comin' in' and instead of 'Lhude sing cuckoo', Pound wrote 'Lhude sing goddam' in his shivering response to the river freezing and his liver quivering.

The tradition of signs pertaining to nature in Ireland has roots which extend back many centuries, not only to the earliest poetry, written in Irish or Latin, but to the ancient Irish myths and legends which preceded the poems.

In Kuno Meyer's *Ancient Irish Poetry*, published nearly a century ago, there appears an English translation of a poem entitled 'Summer is Gone', written in the ninth century, devoted to confirming summer's disappearance:

> My tidings to you: the stag bells,
> Winter snows, summer is gone.
> Wind high and cold, low the sun,
> Short his course, sea running high.
> Deep-red bracken, its shape all gone –
> The wild goose has raised his wanted cry.
> Cold has the wings of birds;
> Season of ice – these are my tidings.

'Summer is Gone' is all about seasonal change. The sun stays lower in the sky. Its short course means shorter days and longer nights. In the summer the ferns are green, but at the end of summer they turn from green to red and slowly disintegrate until May of the following year, when the new fern growth pops out of the soil to begin another cycle.

The early Irish monks who wrote some of the poignant nature poetry had learned about nature from their pagan parents. The perspective the Irish Celts treasured and adhered to was a marvellous synthesis of nature, seasonal change, and their native druidic religion.[5]

The Irish Celts, as well as other European Celts, celebrated four major holidays, all related to nature and to seasonal change. *Imbolc*, the first holiday of our calendar year, but the second of the Celtic cycle, took place about 1 February. This was associated with the advent of spring when ewes were birthing lambs and lactating. This was the time when the earliest spring flowers, such as the primrose, had begun to bloom. It was the start of the crop planting season. This birthing of lambs and plants was filled with feminine energy and, appropriately, the holiday was associated with the Celtic goddess Bridget. She was revered not only by the farmers whose agricultural livelihood was protected by her, but also by poets and smiths. Poets were in tune with seasonal change, and smiths, using magical fires, transformed earth into metal, just as Bridget resurrected the life of spring out of winter's death. It's no wonder the Irish saint, Bridget, is so popular.

Bealtaine, the third holiday of the Celtic cycle, occurred around

1 May, a time when the grass on the mountain-tops had re-vitalised sufficiently for grazing to be resumed. Just as smiths use fire for the transformation of ore into metal, the druids built two fires on *Bealtaine* for the purification of cattle before they were led up the mountain for summer grazing. The cattle were driven between the druids' two bonfires, so that the smoke could work its protective magic. *Bealtaine* is also associated with fertility.

Just as *Bealtaine* followed *Imbolc* by three months, so did *Lughnasa*, the fourth Celtic holiday, follow *Bealtaine*. Lugh was the god who fathered the mighty warrior Cúchulainn, of ancient Irish myths. Lugh was also the god of Harvest. Associated with *Lughnasa*, celebrated about 1 August were the first-fruits feast and the Games of Lugh, where the athletes would compete with one another in the performance of Celtic sports. This was also a time for pan-tribal gatherings.

The first holiday of the Celtic cycle, and the last on our Roman calendar, was *Samhain*. This was a winter event when all the vegetation was dead except for the evergreens and holly. The leaves had fallen off the deciduous trees and were rotting into the earth. The fissures in rocks and the earthen holes which served as corridors for the gods and spirits of the other world to transit back and forth from the human realm, were no longer camouflaged by bracken and briars. At this time of the year these other world beings were closest to humans. That is why *Samhain* was the most scary and dangerous of the four Celtic festivals. *Samhain* was the predecessor of modern day Hallowe'en. This was the night when all the beings of the other world left their usual domain to haunt the human world and play tricks on the unsuspecting. So if you woke up alive as a Celt on 1 November, after a night of the other world beings hovering around, it was a good sign.

Although these ancient Celtic holidays are no longer celebrated as such, nature and other world sensitivity associated with them looms large with those living in rural Ireland.

When one thinks about signs of nature, certain concepts come to mind. Concepts appropriate to signs range from the scientifically empirical to the more purely intuitive and include any number of variations in between.

When I was a Naval Intelligence Officer during my early twenties, the term used was 'indicator'. The sonic profile of a submarine's propeller churning through the Mediterranean Sea was an indicator that it was a Soviet submarine of a specified class.

Moving back to periods in Irish history centuries before the Office of Naval Intelligence was ever even dreamed of, signs, as comprehended by the Old Irish-speaking natives, tended to be subjected to less rigorous empirical analysis. They believed, for example, the *capeen* (little cloud cap) on top of the mountain was a sure sign the gods were angry. Thus, when you seek to understand how an Irishman is interpreting certain signs of nature, it is useful to enquire what species of judgment is being made. Is it a causal understanding? A correlation? An indicator? Or a pronouncement related to perceived machinations being undertaken in the other world?

One day Patrick, one of the men helping us renovate our cottage, noticed a swallow, carrying a reed in its beak, flying into a little opening at the intersection of the roof and west gable wall of the cottage. Looking a bit apprehensive, he declared, 'A house that a bird builds a nest in, is a house that is haunted'.

Connor, Damien de Barra's son, is the nature boy of his family. Connor is a bird and field man. He raises peacocks, doves, carrier pigeons, ducks and other feathered creatures. I have been privileged to hike around the fields with Connor, who has the gift of discerning whether holes in the earth lead to foxes' dens, rabbits' burrows, or neither. To the Kerry farmer, foxes and rabbits bring as much bad news as do disgruntled fairies. In the spring when the vixen has her kits, she kills newborn lambs and drags them back to her den to feed her babies. Rabbits cause a number of problems other than raiding the vegetable garden. Sheep and cattle step into their burrows and can twist or break a leg. Rabbits can also be diseased, and if hunted down by dogs and eaten, can infect the dog. So farmers want to rid themselves of foxes and rabbits.

Connor explained that there are natural enemies of the fox and rabbit, which if skilfully utilised, can save the farmers much grief. Jack Russell terriers were bred, among other reasons, to climb down into fox dens and kill the kits. Every dead fox kit, as the farmers see it, means life is that much safer for the young lambs. Ferrets let loose down rabbit burrows, soon reach the warrens and make short work out of the bunnies. So as a service to his farmer neighbours, young Connor surveys the various animal-created apertures in the earth, looking for signs of foxes and rabbits. Connor noted that last autumn, when a storm blew the door off his birdcage, a fox marched in and killed every one of them.

Another tutor who, sad to say, died a few years ago, was Arthur Bonnel. Arthur, a highly skilled outdoorsman who grew up on a farm in England, had years ago moved to Kerry where he literally lived off the land. He kept a very productive vegetable garden, and with his black labrador retriever, Raq, would hunt and fish all over the Kerry woodlands. Sometimes Arthur would take me with him on such outings, but he soon gave up doing so because I would inadvertently make so much noise and commotion when I hiked around with him that I would scare into hiding any possible game located in the immediate vicinity. So Arthur chose, instead, to sacrifice hunting and fishing when he took me for walks with him through the wilds of Kerry.

I recall the first hike I took with Arthur through Killarney National Park. We were slogging through bogland in our wellies. I was a bit apprehensive about sinking into the marshes and drowning, but Arthur kept walking on with great confidence. He was following deer tracks. The deer feel the earth through their hooves, which pick up vibrations about whether it is solid or marshy ground they are treading on. He said that often, while hunting, he would see a herd of deer run at a gallop through the bogs. Arthur, God rest his soul, could detect the freshness of a deer track as easily as he could that of a deer dropping.

Arthur also helped me gain some introductory knowledge about ecology. While walking with me through the Killarney National Park one day, Arthur explained that the wood mouse, bank vole and pygmy shrew, all small mammals, are snatched as prey by swooping predator birds such as the kestrel and a number of owl species. Similarly, mammal predators such as the fox, stoat, brown rat and pine marten will feed on nesting baby birds and the adult parents too, whenever they find such prey. Arthur also pointed out that recent overgrazing by sheep and by the imported Japanese deer in the park has substantially lowered the insect population, which in turn has cut back somewhat on one of the birds' main sources of food supply. All of these relationships between species and kingdoms seem often more intricate than one would expect, particularly if that one were as ignorant about the ways of nature as I. My Irish-American grandfather used to say, 'The admission of ignorance can become the beginning of wisdom, but don't hold out hope in all cases.'

I began to comprehend that the way all these people came to fathom the mysteries of nature and her manifold signs was through adoption of an approach different from my busy, goal-directed mentality. They somehow had learned to cultivate a mental stillness, out of which receptivity was made possible. For only in being quiet of mind could they attain the openness of spirit to allow nature's signs to present themselves. Only in such a mind state could they begin to recognise nature's patterns. Such recognition proceeds from an agenda-less noticing.

Instead of launching a quest after nature's mysteries my mentors, in their stillness, had seriously allowed nature to impress herself and her signs upon them.

A few years ago, while walking through a meadow on our land down by the sea, I saw a cow standing in the shade of an oak tree, licking the moisture off its still womb-wet calf. Less than minutes old, the heifer calf was standing on its wobbly legs as its mother ran her tongue all over its back and flanks. Long before the mother cow stopped licking her new baby, it banged mama's udder with a hard head-butt and began to suck milk.

The next morning I noticed a stuck sack of placenta hanging down four feet beneath the tired mother's tail. That baby calf kept up its udder butts, apparently trying to suck its mama dry. Next, the calf walked six feet to sniff me, seemed satisfied, then lay right down. I lay down next to her, looked into her curious eyes, and smiled.

Soon the farmer came to lead the cow into another pasture that was easier for the vet to access. As we neared the road the calf refused to budge. I lifted her up, like holding a house cat, crossed the road, and set her down when her mother mooed. And off she ran. Then strangely, later in the day, I heard the calf bleating, not in the pasture where she had been taken, but in the same place where she had been born, which was where she had sniffed me the day before. The baby calf had easily stepped through the rails of the fence, making her way back to the exact location where, two days before, she had entered the world.

In late October I heard the stag's mating call. At this time of year rutted whistling fills the humid night air with eeriness. That shrill keening bouncing off each forest tree comes not from banshees, gnomes or fairies, but from quivering bucks bent on seducing does in estrus. That persistent two-note primal stag song courses through darkness, starts womb-deep stirring.

I was beginning to become still and receptive enough to allow nature's subtle messages to penetrate my waking consciousness.

I experienced another intriguing adventure involving animal noises. It occurred as I was climbing up Skellig Michael, an island just west of the Iveragh Peninsula. The puffin, an auk, looks something like a miniature penguin, but with a large orange and yellow parrot-like beak and brighter orange webbed feet and legs. They nest in colonies all over Skellig Michael. I have been there at least a half dozen times before, whereupon I noticed that puffins burrow into the earth to make their nests. I hadn't previously noticed a bullfrog-like sound coming out of their burrows. It was hard to believe that the puffin could make such a noise. Yet I knew it wasn't a bullfrog making all that racket.

When I returned home to conduct further research on this peculiar feathered creature, upon turning to *The Complete Guide to Ireland's Birds*, I read: 'A normally silent species. However, in breeding burrows, puffins can be heard to give low, moaning, growling *arr-ow-arr* calls.' The book also mentioned that at such breeding sites the puffin can often be seen returning from feeding forays with up to ten sand-eels draped crosswise on its bill.

From time to time I give myself a small pat on the back for noticing something unusual about an animal's behaviour, such as the bullfrog-like noises of the puffin. Perhaps my fondest discovery involving birds pertained to the fulmar, a relation of the seagull. Last year while visiting Cape Clear, I saw fulmars up close for the first time. Cape Clear is the southernmost point of Irish territory, an island just south of the Cork port of Baltimore. I walked to the edge of a one-hundred-and-fifty foot cliff dropping down to the sea. Hundreds of fulmars nested along the long cliff-top ridge of stone. I sat still for about two hours watching the fulmars take off and glide around the swirls of ocean air currents.

Previously, for some reason, I had believed that every animal's occupational undertakings consisted only of hunting, feeding, fighting, sleeping and reproducing. They seemed inherently incapable of pure recreation. Yet, from watching the fulmars closely, I noticed that they were exercising none of these survival skills. Instead, they were like surfers riding the big waves. Only these were air currents, not waves.

I would watch one fulmar's entire flight with rapture. It would jump off the cliff, spread its wings, catch an upwelling air current and simply ride it, by banking its wings to make turns. When the bird had been airborne for four or five minutes, it would navigate with spread wings back to its landing platform and then fold its feathers along its back and watch its buddies perform. I thought to myself, this bird has his priorities straight. It's not all work and no play for the fulmar.

I owe most of my neophyte knowledge of nature not to my own limited powers of observation, but rather to Denis Casey, who to this day is unable to grasp why I don't know more than I do. Denis has patiently explained the same things for years, and somehow I seem to forget so much of what he says. Nature comes naturally to Denis and I am beginning to see nature the way he does: through signs, sometimes associated with seasonal change or growth cycles, and sometimes not.

Kenmare is adjacent to where the Roughty River suddenly broadens out into the Kenmare Bay. Just before the Roughty widens into the bay, it passes through a very narrow ford over which a bridge was constructed in the nineteenth century. One spring evening, I noticed a seal in the ford, treading water against the incoming tide. Oblivious to the obvious purpose of the seal's chosen location, I asked Denis why it had selected the ford, of all places, to bob around the water's surface.

Looking at me as if he were speaking to a young child, Denis said, 'Jaysus, David, all the salmon headed up the Roughty or for the Sheen River have to pass through this ford. The seal knows they are running now. So he just waits here for them to swim into his mouth for dinner. A seal swimming in the ford is a sure sign the salmon are running'.

The next morning Denis asked, 'Did you see the swallow's nest built up near the eaves of the house? Yesterday evening the mother swallow was sitting on her nest, which meant she was waiting for her baby birds to hatch. Now this is very late in the summer for her to be having baby birds. They'll never be strong enough to fly to Africa by autumn of this year. They'll never make it.'

Another lesson along similar lines that Denis taught me, one I was able to remember the first time I heard it, related to the broken mussel shells that I would find on the rocky point of our land which forms a small peninsula jutting westwardly into Kenmare Bay. I couldn't understand how these broken mussel shells got deposited on the rocks. Denis explained: 'An oyster-catcher, a bird that lives off shellfish, flies up in the air and drops them on the rocks, which breaks the shells open. Then the oyster-catcher flies down to feast on his dinner of fresh raw mussels. Often the oystercatcher just hammers the shells with his tough beak and breaks them open that way. The otter does basically the same thing. He climbs out of the water onto the rocks, smacks the mussel shell against the stone and swallows the contents down his gullet.' Broken mussel shells are a sign that the oys-tercatcher or otter has been a recent visitor. I haven't yet asked Denis if he can discern, by the state of the evidence, which of these two mussel-eating species has deposited the broken shells.

Denis is just as good at reading plant signs. Another spring day, he was transplanting into larger pots little birch saplings that he had placed into smaller pots the previous year, having dug them out of the ground. Denis showed me how in both the smaller and larger pots he had placed rich dark soil interspersed with sand. 'You see,' he said, showing me the saplings' root struc-ture, 'when you put a load of sand in the pots it makes these little fellows work harder to grow roots through the un-nurturing sand into the richer soil. That way, when you finally plant them back in the earth, their long roots will straightaway dig them-selves into the soil, and the birch trees will grow a lot faster.' Before I could respond, Denis added, 'long straggly roots like this are a sure sign that the sapling has been digging its roots through sand searching for richer soil. If you put saplings in rich soil from the start, the roots have no need to grow. They merely suck up the nourishment which is already there for them, and then don't develop strong root systems.'

Four years ago Denis taught me another lesson. We were putting up barbed-wire fencing using pre-treated, kiln-dried fence posts. As we strung the fence along, we came to a hollow that was too deep for the standard-sized fence post to do us much good. The earth-moving machine that had extended our driveway up towards the main road had knocked over two or three trees that had been in the way. I learned from Denis that the species of tree involved was popularly called the sallee. Denis took his chainsaw to a long branch with a four-inch diameter, cleaning off all the little branches. When he finished with his chainsaw we had a twelve-foot length of sallee. 'Here is your stake,' Denis announced. 'We'll pop her in the ground and she'll do fine. Sallees make great stakes, you know. They'll grow back into trees, particularly if you plant them upside down.'

I knew that Denis must have been kidding, because everybody knows that a twelve-foot pole stuck in the ground is never going to do anything but rot in time. So I just said, 'Right, Denis, whatever you say.' Much to my surprise when I returned to Ireland the next summer and inspected the fence line, there was the sallee stake that Denis had made, full of new little branches all sprouting green leaves. One would have thought I might have caught on, but I didn't.

Just recently Denis and I were working in another pasture on our land, putting in fence posts and planting trees. Having set the fence posts and attaching two strands of barbed wire to them, Denis positioned the pine saplings he had earlier grown from cuttings, while I started to dig the holes into which he would plant the young trees. Noticing that I knew not what I was doing, even pertaining to the digging of a simple nine-inch hole in the ground, Denis helpfully suggested, 'Cut a circle in the ground a little bigger than a dinner plate with your shovel. Then dig all around the circle you made until you can lift out the circular sod. Then lift it out of its hole, turn it over, cut a single slice from the centre to its rim. Next, using your pick, loosen up each hole where the sod had been, and I'll follow you along and be planting the trees.'

As Denis pulled the young trees out of their pots, he was careful to avoid damaging the roots while he tugged at them gently so they would more easily spread themselves out in the rich soil where they were being planted. Then he took the upside-down sods and placed one around each sapling by slipping the sod around the trunk along the slice I had cut. 'This way,' he said, 'the sod will keep the weeds away and let the roots dig right into the soil without any competition.'

When we finished the planting and were getting ready to clean up and return our tools back to the storage shed, I noticed that Denis was cutting a branch off a tree which would have stolen too much sunlight from the last sapling he had planted. 'Is that a sallee tree you're cutting?' I asked.

'It is, and so are those other three trees that are lined up with this one. They must have been used as fence posts forty or fifty years ago, and now they are thirty feet high.'

The first of the sallees we came to had a dried end of the original stake protruding out from the centre of the trunk of the tree where it had branched out, forming the two major limbs.

Later in the day, having thought about all that Denis had taught me concerning nature over the past fifteen years, I recalled his lessons on the seasons, on cuttings, on the alkaline or acid soil preference of each plant, on preferences for sun or shade, damp or drier ground as best to thrive in, as well as hundreds of other bits of ecological information. I felt I was finally beginning to shed most of my city boy stupidity and at last was beginning to acquire the mind of a true nature lover.

There was one little discovery that I was proud to have recently made. I wanted to raise it with Denis. It concerned my observation that nearly every non-cultivated holly tree I had ever seen was crowded in beneath larger trees above it, which absorbed most of the light and probably most of the nutrients out of the soil. I asked Denis, 'Why does the holly tree always seem to select such miserable and un-ideal locations in which to grow, all jammed up close to and under larger trees above them?'

Denis looked at me with a sympathetic twinkle in his eye and answered, 'Holly trees don't select such locations at all. The birds select the locations by eating holly berries. They go sit on branches of trees, and where their droppings fall is where the holly trees grow.'

As earlier suggested, it requires a stillness in the soul to become receptive enough to notice nature's signs. There is a mystery to signs. Signs point. Signs portend. Signs are often omens.

When one assimilates an aggregate of nature's signs, one is pointed toward a larger realm. That is toward the Order of Nature, the Cosmic Order and the Order of Being. There are mysteries that cannot easily be understood by the rational, cognitive mind. Rather, only hints of these mysteries can be grasped. That finding or intuiting is done with the mind of a poet, like the Irish medieval poet-monks who could hear what animals were telling them.

To conclude this chapter I should mention the time I saw an otter climb up out of the bay onto our land and walk over to Sarah, who was doing her QiGong meditative exercises under a tree quite close to the water. The otter got within four feet of Sarah, stood up on its hind legs, looked right at her and started talking. I heard the chattering sound the otter was making. Sarah just continued with her exercise, her eyes looking back lovingly at the otter. When she finished her practice, they had a conversation together.

Perhaps I shouldn't have mentioned this latter incident at all, because its inclusion may be a sure sign that I am certifiable as well as ignorant!

SENSE OF PLACE

Not only do many rural Irish seem to possess an acute sensitivity to nature, but they often also acquire a deep bonding to place. It is as if a part of their soul is attached to the land on which they were reared. The bond is even more intensive than that. It is as if a strand of their soul seems not only knotted to the physical ground on which they walk, but also to its history. The rural Irish seem to absorb a knowledge of, and find common identity with, those long dead who walked the land. Such persons include not only family members and relatives – ancestral and living – but also others who have somehow imprinted themselves upon the land.

The *where* of a person is so linked to the *who* that, if severed, the *who* would collapse into a substanceless state. It is virtually as if the most critical component of their identity is inseparably linked to the land or place. This could, and often does, include the house in which the person was raised. It can include a house in which an ancestor lived and to which the person feels a continuing strong attachment. So strong it sometimes transcends comprehensibility.

A friend of mine, who grew up on the east coast of Ireland,

bought a run down house in County Kerry, which he restored with great care. It was originally owned by the grandfather of a local acquaintance of my friend. That acquaintance, who had visited his grandfather in the house as a child some forty years earlier, had acquired some sort of possessive interest in his grandfather's house. At some level of his consciousness he seemed to feel that he had more of a proprietorial right to the house than my friend who had legally bought it at fair market value. The acquaintance so obsessively resented any outsider living in the house his grandfather had once owned, that one evening when he walked out of a pub, he noticed my friend passing by, then glared at him and snarled, 'You know it's my grandfather's house that you're living in'.

This sort of experience might not be a common occurrence. But neither would it be a rarity. In rural Ireland, one discovers that most persons have acquired a deep linkage to the land. And with it a sense of place that can nearly be compared to a migratory bird, like a swallow, returning many thousands of miles each spring to the nest at which it had roosted the previous year. This highly localised sense of place not only lasts one's entire life, but is literally taken to the grave. When one examines the gravestones in local cemeteries, one usually finds the name of the person carved in the stone and directly beneath it three other names. These are in descending order, the name of the smallest location, the name of the local townland and finally, the name of the town or village. The smallest location is sometimes termed sub-denomination of the townland. It could have precisely delineated boundaries. But sometimes boundaries are vague and without any exact delineation. Yet that piece of land, however difficult to define, is known to all persons who dwell within it and it is the piece of land with which they have the closest identity.

Beneath the name of the deceased and the three lines related to place will usually appear the dates of birth and death. You won't often see 'Jack Kelly, famous hurler', or for that matter any information about who that person was. The only other likely inscription would be RIP, meaning Rest in Peace. Thus, the story on the gravestone is that the real *who* of the person is told by describing the *where* or *place* of the person. *Place* outranks occupation or any other biographical data. The tale of the tombstone is that one's claim to fame lies in one's *place*.

This identification with place is so acute that in rural Ireland there are no house numbers. Persons are so linked to their place that no house numbers are needed. Where a person is from is often more important than the person's occupation, character and reputation.

This Irish sense of place is so subtle its detection is difficult for foreign visitors. But it is so vitally strong because, like so many other aspects of Irish culture, its roots are ancient and indestructible. Coming to understand this almost mythic sense of place became a near obsession for me. I sought to engage myself in a series of adventures that might, if successfully executed, expand and clarify my understanding of this phenomenon that had, over the millennia, become so deeply embedded in the rural Irish psyche.

How was I to penetrate this elusive mystery? My neighbour, Mickey Ned, the footballer, introduced me to the parish priest, Tom Looney. Tom happened to be not only a scholar of Irish cultural traditions, but an aficionado of their preservation. Mickey Ned assured me that Fr Tom could answer all my questions including why it is that so many living Irish people I have met seem to know the names of all the nearby stone circles and other archaeological ruins, mountains, valleys, ravines, outcrops, rivers, streams and natural springs, as well as the place names of smaller sites dotted all over the local landscape.

Tom Looney invited me to meet him at the presbytery for a strategy session. As we sat in his living-room, enjoying a cup of tea, we began to discuss the inter-related subjects that had so vigorously stimulated my curiosity.

'How did you become aware of the Irishman's strong sense of place?' he asked.

'My late friend the artist, Michael Sheehan, who returned to Ireland for his retirement, served for nearly twenty years as a correspondent for an Irish American newspaper in New York, *The Irish World and American Industrial Liberator and Gaelic American*. Michael gave me a selection of his favourite columns that he had written for that paper. Michael always linked each character to a highly localised place, such as a townland, or sub-townland, rather than a larger territorial unit such as a village, town or county. He would comment on the lore and traditions by naming distinguished persons or historical events associated with the place. The same seems to be true of the weekly newspapers published throughout Ireland and the local radio stations. Each person mentioned is usually identified by his or her town and townland.'

'Did you ever hear of the Irish word *Dinnseanchas* (pronounced dinn shan'a cus)?' Tom read aloud from one of his many books, '*Dinnseanchas* – a topographical tract in Middle Irish prose and verse giving the legendary history and the etymology of the names of remarkable hills, mounds, caves, cairns, cromlechs, raths, duns, plains, lakes, rivers, estuaries, islands and so forth. It takes its name from *dind* or *dinn*, a fortified hill, and *seanchas*, a history.'[6]

The original *Dinnseanchas*, I learned from Tom, was an early medieval tract and over the centuries it became known as the name of any tract that deals with the description and traditions of a given place. *Dinnseanchas* means, essentially, the study of the lore of a place, including all that has been written or known about it over the years, as well as its legends and place names passed on by word of mouth from generation to generation.

'Why is place so important to the Irish?' I asked, searching for a more concrete handle with which to grasp this topic.

'Historically the Irish Celts were a tribal or clannish people. *Tuath* (pronounced two'ah), meaning the people, was the name given to the tribe or clan to which one belonged. Irish myth and tradition stresses the importance of one's roots in the *Tuath*. Your identity was not only yourself as an individual. It was just as much the people you came from and the place where they lived. That was true of the Irish Celts and could have been true of Irish Stone Age and Bronze Age people, too.'

'What about the matter of how ancient writing about place began in Ireland, Tom?'

'Did you ever hear of Ogham (pronounced ohm)?'

'I did, if you mean the coded alphabet often found on early Irish Christian gravestones or boundary markers.'

'Some say it was used for other purposes as well. I'm no scholar but if I had to guess, I'd say Ogham, or some kind of writing, may well pre-date Christianity in Ireland, and it could also be used for other forms of writing than gravestones and boundary markings alone.'

Tom next asked me if I had ever heard of *Pluais na Scríoba*.

(pronounced Plu as na Scree o ba). 'It means Cave of the Writing. There is a two thousand foot high mountain near Lauragh by the name of Caha, part of the Caha chain that separates Kerry and Cork. At the top of that mountain is a cave full of some kind of ancient writing.

'If you take a hike up that mountain, you could see for yourselves the Cave of the Writing, touch its wall that Stone or Bronze Age man may have written upon, and at the same time learn more about the meaning of *Dinnseanchas*. Now you ring Stephen O'Shea, one of my parishioners who is a real expert on local lore and place. He knows all about *Pluais na Scríoba*. Stephen will take you to see the Cave of the Writing. Moses climbed the mountain and came down with the Ten Commandments. You can climb the mountain and come down with knowledge of the mysterious writing. Let me know how it goes, and good luck to you.'

One of the reasons I have come to admire Tom Looney is that he not only has an intense curiosity about matters of cultural tradition but he also has a solid knowledge of, and commitment to, preserving an awareness of these matters among his parishioners. Each year he conducts an *Éigse* (pronounced egg'-sha), or special teaching, in the form of a two- or three-day conference which focuses on a particular local place or tradition and seeks to explore its roots. Tom explains that, due largely to television, interest among the Irish in their history and traditions has begun to wane, and the sense of place and respect for its local lore, kept alive for centuries by the *seanchaí* may soon disappear from consciousness.

In rural Ireland business is done through connections. It was largely due to the connection with Tom Looney, that Stephen O'Shea, his teenage, mountain goat-like son Liam, and his son's Jack Russell terrier, Spot, all agreed to escort my visiting godson Joseph, my friend Denis, and me up a vertical climb of two thousand feet to explore the cave.

Stephen O'Shea, born and raised near the village of Lauragh in Kerry, had moved to Dublin in his early twenties to work as a carpenter. After eighteen years in Dublin, the call to return to Kerry and all the familiar mountains, valleys, rivers, lakes and assorted arcane, but familiar, place names grew mightily in Stephen's memory so much so that one day about eight years ago, he couldn't any longer bear being separated from his roots. So he packed up his family and returned to his farm near Lauragh and began again to raise cattle and sheep.

As we trekked up the mountain Stephen pointed to a rock that looked like a human silhouette perched at the top of a cliff located on the north side of Caha Mountain and said, 'That rock is named *Fear Bréige* (pronounced fear' braig gah). It means something that looks like a man but isn't really. It has been called that for as long as Irish has been spoken in this land.'

Denis said that everyone knows about all the places near where they grow up. He then explained how early in the eighteenth century, a local man cut off a priest's head and delivered it on a platter to anti-Catholic Protestants who paid the murderer a bounty. He named the families in the area whose members died during the famine and are interred in the local burial ground next to the ruin of a sixth-century church founded by St Finian.

About an hour – and a lot more sweat – later, we made it to *Pluais na Scríoba*. It consisted of a sandstone boulder the size of a thirty-five foot cubed block, with another slice of sandstone thirty-five feet square and about eight feet thick resting up against the larger block, creating a lean-to effect. This large stone lean-to had probably resulted from glacial action which occurred perhaps fifteen thousand years ago.

Liam announced that the writing was located on the wall of the larger block of stone which was protected by the smaller slice of stone leaning against it. We had arrived at a place full of mystery, known to the local farmers whose sheep grazed on Caha Mountain, but not contained on our official Ordnance Survey map.

I told Joseph, 'This is no ordinary cave. This is a cave that contains a special and hardly known kind of writing that could have been used by Stone Age or Bronze Age man. There are probably not more than four or five other caves like this in the entire world.'

Stephen politely suggested that a professor from Cork had seen what was on the wall of the cave, denied that it was writing at all, and dismissed it as simply a place where some men long ago had been sharpening their knives. 'I know nothing about Ogham or any other kind of ancient writing, but the marks on the wall look as if they were put there for a purpose other than sharpening knives. Let's take a look and ye can see for yourselves.'

We stepped into the cave and I began to take pictures of this strange writing that did look a lot like Ogham. There were stem lines which seemed to be natural fractures in the stone with vertical parallel marks above and below. We sat on the floor of the cave looking at the writing and running our fingertips in the grooves cut into the stone.

As we stepped out of the cave, Stephen pointed to a nearby marshy hollow and said that place is known as *Loch Charraig na Scríobe* (pronounced Loch Har na Scree o ba), the Lake of the Rock of the Engravings. In the winter it is full of water.

We began our descent, taking a smoother but more circuitous route, first down the mountain and then around it, following the river bed. Stephen pointed out the ruins of two houses with long gone roofs. 'The great grandchildren of the people who once were farmers living here long ago now own shops in Kenmare.'

On the way back I realised that in the course of our tour Stephen had pointed out every feature of the landscape, natural or man made, and had given us its name and history. In one sense, we had seen land, the owners of which currently held a deed conveying to them legal title to that land. In that sense it was merely earth and rock, grass and reeds, dry or boggy.

But in another sense, we had seen a living stage on which a successive stream of representatives from each era of Irish history had lived. An invisible cord, fashioned out of ethnic vibrations, linked Stephen to each of those representatives and to the land on which they walked.

Less than a week after Joseph headed home to America, my octagenarian friend, Bill Grant, a Celtic scholar at the University of Edinburgh, arrived for a two-day visit. Bill and I met through our annual summer meetings at Maynooth, County Kildare, where the Irish Medieval Society convenes to present scholarly papers and quaff gallons of Guinness. I showed Bill the pictures I had taken of the Cave of the Writing. Bill nearly jumped out of his chair with enthusiasm. 'This writing has got to be proto-Ogham,' he said, explaining how earlier Ogham, like early Hebrew, was written in consonants only. 'Can you get me a couple of sets of these photos so I can send them on to an Irish Ogham expert, and to another one at Harvard? I think you have a major find that could date back twenty-five hundred to three thousand years BC. What's more, I suspect this writing, if I'm correct, may help establish a number of critically important principles. First, it would demonstrate that proto-Ogham was used in Ireland. Second, it could establish that proto-Ogham was used for purposes other than for boundary and tombstone writing. This writing you photographed in the cave is perhaps a prayer to a local fertility deity. Third, it may help boost the fusionist theory of writing – that late Stone Age and Bronze Age people learned about writing from traders who travelled from country to country, rather than inventing it solely by themselves within Ireland, as the isolationists contend. I'll send you a letter with more about this as soon as I get back to Edinburgh.'

Two weeks later Bill's letter arrived. In it he requested that I ask Fr Looney and Stephen not to let anybody put chalk marks on the writing on the cave, because that would prevent scholars from digging out microscopic samples from the creases in the writing which could accurately establish the date of the writing at the cave. Bill also sent pictures showing Ogham writing in America at two locations in West Virginia believed to have been inscribed by Ireland's St Brendan or by his monks in the sixth century, over a thousand years before Christopher Columbus took his first breath. Bill also sent a lot of information on the fusionist/isolationist debate over origins of Ogham. He said that as soon as he received a response from the experts to the photos I sent him, he would let me know. Also, he indicated that he wanted to climb the mountain and see the Cave of the Writing for himself. In his early eighties Bill climbed a several hundred foot high mountain in Edinburgh three times a week, without use of ropes and other rock climbing gear. Although a group of scholars, later organised by Bill, visited the cave, they departed as baffled about the strange writing as we had been.

I felt a need to know more about *Dinnseanchas*, so I went to see Breandán Ó Cíobháin (pronounced O'Kee vaghn) whom Fr Looney had recommended as Ireland's leading expert on that subject. He lives in a small town called Ventry, or Ceann Trá in Irish, near Dingle.

I drove to the Dingle Peninsula and saw again some of its most famous archaeological sites: Dún Beg, a Neolithic fort; the Riasc gravestone from the sixth century; Gallarus Oratory, a corbelled stone seventh- or eighth-century church still in perfect condition; and Kilmalkerdar church, an Irish Romanesque structure, now a ruin, built in the twelfth century. Soon after arriving at his home in Ventry, I asked Breandán what he knew about the Cave of the Writing. He said that while he knew of its existence, he had not yet finished his field work on the Beara Peninsula, and perhaps we could climb Caha Mountain and explore it together some time.

As we sat on his back patio with a splendid view of Ventry Harbour, I asked him to explain the aetiology of the highly developed Irish sense of place. He answered, 'You couldn't have come to a better place to get a feel for that,' pointing to a beach in the centre of Ventry Harbour and a mountain behind it. He explained that some of the most popular legends in Irish literature, whose roots extend well beyond a thousand years, are based upon a king named Fionn MacCumhail (pronounced Finn Mac-Cool) and the Fianna, his army of warriors who loved to fight battles and hunt deer. These legends are known as the Fenian Cycle, one of three major cycles or clusters of Irish legends. Fionn MacCumhail and his Fianna were real people who lived in Ireland long before history began to be recorded. According to Breandán, 'The Dingle Peninsula is one of the major sites in which the legends take place, and there are place names all over the peninsula that correspond to many of the tales recorded in the Fenian Cycle. That mountain over there is called *Cruach Mharthain* (pronounced Crow Vawrhin). At the base of its southern slope is Ventry Harbour, where one of Fionn's major battles took place. Fionn had stationed members of his Fianna at various lookout stations all along the coast of Ireland, including one at the top of Cruach Mharthain. The lookouts were to watch for any signs of invading fleets approaching Ireland. The name of the man stationed at the top of that mountain over there was Conn Crithir (pronounced Conn Kree er), and the place at the summit is to this day named *Leaba* (pronounced Lay bah) *Conn Crithir*, meaning the bed of Conn Crithir.

'Conn fell asleep on watch, and while he slept the invading force of Daire Donn (pronounced Dare Dunn), king of the world, landed in Ventry Harbour and began its attack. Conn Crithir woke to the din of battle, actually more of a one-sided slaughter, as Daire Donn's warriors were killing the local inhabitants and stealing their cattle, and gathering up whatever else they could to feed the army of invaders. Conn Crithir leaped down the mountain. It took him three leaps to reach the shore where the invasion had taken place. When I was a boy here in Ventry, my pals and I would go up the mountain in search of the three ridges Conn was supposed to have landed on during his leaps down the mountain. But we could never find them, no matter how hard we looked, even though they were named in the legend.

'There is another site in the slight hollow part-way down the slope of the same mountain, that is also part of the Fenian legends. The hollow is called *Leaba Dhiarmada is Ghráinne* (pronounced Laba Yeermud iss Yrawnya). You've heard of the elopement of Diarmuid and Gráinne?'

Breandán explained, 'Diarmuid's surname was Ó Duibhne (pronounced O'Div na), which is the name of the people who then populated the Dingle Peninsula, named after the goddess Duibhne. That name has been found on four Ogham stones dating back at least fifteen hundred years. Diarmuid, who was a member of the Fianna, fell in love with Gráinne, the daughter of Cormac MacAirt, the king of Ireland, who had been promised to Fionn, Cormac's leading general in charge of the Fianna. Diarmuid eloped with Gráinne and headed west from Tara to his own homelands on the Dingle Peninsula. In the hollow up there he slept with Gráinne, just below the peak of the mountain you can see from here.'

Breandán continued, 'As a result of the Normans settling in Dingle, the place names here are a hybrid. The first element is Celtic, which created place names in the Irish language, and the second element is Norman, which reflects Norman surnames and culture. The surname of one of the Norman families that settled here was Trant, who built a castle nearby called Caheratrant (pronounced Ca huru trant). It means the fort of Trant which survived until the last century, when people took the stones to build houses in the village.

'I started working on place names thirty-five years ago. In the mountain and coastal areas, there is a fantastic residue of tradition and place names, even amongst people who do not speak Irish. They still know the Irish place names. Many older people knew the legends of names that have been passed down from generation to generation.

'Most of the place names were on mountains and coasts because of the density of population. In the north of Kerry where there were bigger holdings, the names there had petered out because the population density was so low. When you have distinctive features on the landscape, and people who have a need to identify minute points of land, you end up with pragmatic place names. If you lost a sheep on a mountain and a neighbour saw it somewhere, he would just mention such a name, like 'Viking Rock' for example. This system was based upon special features of the land. Likewise if a farmer was working on a mountain in heavy fog knowing the distinctive features of the landscape enabled him to make his way safely down the mountain.'

I told Breandán that the mystery of the Irishman's powerful identity with place has been intriguing me for years.

'It's hard to distinguish the things that come together when we discuss sense of place. I told you about the famous battle of Fionn MacCumhail versus the king of the world. From that prehistoric event a lot of what happened during it somehow seems to hang on to the land itself. The place names tell us that.

'It's hard to say what gives Irish people a sense of place. The funny thing is that even Irish people who have left Ireland or moved from their rural childhood homes to the cities still retain their sense of place, through names associated with their family as it goes back. They have a strong personal attachment to place. I can see it all the time.'

Before I knew it, I had spent five hours with this man who had such an extraordinary understanding of the roots of his country's culture.

On the way back to Beara Peninsula, I thought about his acute awareness of the powerful sense of place. Before I left, Breandán showed me his Volkswagon van that he had modified into a camper of sorts. He had driven it nearly two hundred thousand miles around Ireland in search of place names and the lore associated with them. Ireland's coastal roads all strung together in a circumference would barely exceed a thousand miles. Figuratively speaking, Breandán had onomastically rattled his VW around that track about two hundred times, and he keeps coming back for more.

Recalling all the gravestones I had seen which fixate on *where*, to the neglect of *who*, I wondered if some day someone would dare to inscribe an epitaph on Breandán's gravestone which would read: 'Here lies the man who spent his life proving that *who* is really *where*!'

As I drove along returning to South Kerry, I began to wonder if Mickey Ned could explain how playing the games of Irish football and hurling might contribute to a person's sense of place. Mickey Ned O'Sullivan captained the All-Ireland Champion Kerry football team in the mid 1970s, teaches physical education at an Irish-speaking school in County Cork, and spends about 90 per cent of his spare time coaching Gaelic football. Even though he almost never misses going to Mass at Fr Looney's church, you could say that for Mickey Ned, Gaelic football is in itself a religion. Mickey Ned invited me to his home overlooking Kenmare Bay to discuss the linkage between football, hurling, and a close identity with place.

Mickey Ned told me that the Gaelic Athletic Association was formed in 1884 and organised itself on Ireland's thirty-two counties structure, or on a parish by parish basis. In Kerry there are about seventy parishes, and each has its own football team, and most have hurling teams as well.

At the outset the national football championship was determined by a playoff system in which the best parish teams in each county competed for the honour of becoming champions of their particular province. The winning parish team from each of the four provinces competed for the All-Ireland Championship. Some years ago, in order to upgrade the quality of the All-Ireland Championship, the counties went to an all-star system which selected the best players in each county, on the basis of their performance for their parish teams. He continued, 'People identify with success and disassociate with failure. So at both the parish and county level the people want their team to become the winner. This leads to both a greater identification with one's county, as well as with one's own home parish, not only among the players but with the fans as well.

'People in Kerry began to expect success and now they demand it. The closer to the county border, the more avid the fans. You have seen all the Kerry flags along the road near our borders with Cork and Limerick, and when you cross the boundary you see the Cork and Limerick flags flying. You have to stand up and be counted. At the border areas many people from both counties usually drink at the same pubs, and when a football match is coming up between the two, there is much excitement and a lot of talk about who has the best team. Over the years this enthusiasm for one's parish and county teams reinforces one's sense of place.

'Matt the Thrasher, in the novel *Knocknagow*, was a famous weight thrower in the nineteenth century in County Tipperary. He was competing against the English champion hammer thrower. The Englishman had bested Matt twice for the greatest distance. There was only one throw left. When a member of Matt's parish yelled out at him, "Do it for the parish!" Matt dug deep, steeled himself and made a record-breaking throw to win the contest. When asked about how he won, Matt said, "I did it for the parish".

'Our Kenmare team had a serious game today with another Kerry parish, near Tralee. Even though we lost, 8 to 6, the amount of passion that was generated was beyond belief. This identification with Kenmare is phenomenal. Most of these players are living in either Dublin or Cork, and they all come back every week to play for their own home town. None of these players, who are based away from home, play for the teams near where they now live. This same thing is going on in thousands of clubs all over the country. There is an exodus every weekend, just to come home to play with their club. They put everything aside so they never let their club down.

'To be a footballer or a hurler for one's county or parish, at any level, is the emotional and psychic equivalent of being selected to become one of the warriors for the ancient Fianna. You cannot separate the person from the land and the people. They are all one.'

At the end of John B. Keane's *The Bodhrán Makers*, the protagonist leaves Kerry to go to England in search of work. 'He knew that wherever he went or however he might fare he would always be part of what he was leaving.'

It was now after midnight. I just let that awareness sink in and stay with me as I drove back to my house. Then I recalled the poem 'Follower' by Seamus Heaney about the influence his father had on him when he was a little boy, following his father as he tilled the soil. But most of all, it seemed to be about the magical bond and identity with the land that his father treasured so deeply in his heart, which in turn became grafted to Seamus' own soul. The last line of the poem is: 'But today it is my father who keeps stumbling behind me, and will not go away.'

It is ironic in a sense that when we die, whatever it was that constituted the physically recognisable *who* of *what* we were, rots and therefore merges with the *where* of *what* we were. Going back to the *where*, and all the ritual associated with it, is one of the most intense experiences you could possibly have in rural Ireland. If your county wins an All-Ireland football championship, that would be the equivalent of receiving a hundred emotional volts. But funerals can deliver a thousand emotional jolts.

A SPECIAL WAY TO DIE

A man I'll call Eoin died just two weeks before he was to receive a prestigious award in Dublin for his uilleann pipes compositions. The rumour circulating around was that he poisoned himself. Not likely, people were saying, that a mere accident or foul play caused his mid-life death. What is it that drives a man to take his own life?

There is a branch of theology, known as theodicy, which seeks to explain away the existence of evil and injustice in a perfect world created by a loving God. Severe depression cannot easily be explained away. I never met Eoin. I may not ever have even recognised him playing his pipes in the pubs I have visited. But I know that depression was his life-long albatross; and that he had been selected as the first living piper ever to be honoured with such a distinguished award. Eoin, like so many depressed Irish, seemed to have been born under a black cloud that never went away.

I once heard a woman from the west of Ireland say that depression is a cross Jesus gives certain chosen ones to bear through life, so they may better understand the Lord's own suffering. Is it Jesus who directly deals out doses of depression, or rather just a legacy of the gene pool? To what extent is depression induced by tragic events and a miserable family environment? How much of it is due to a character or a body chemistry unfit to overcome it? How much of it is due to the weather with all those ominous dark clouds and never-ending rain, compounded by those long black winter nights?

Strange, isn't it, the cards we are dealt? We come into this world facing the luck of the DNA draw, spawned by our parents, oblivious at the moment of conception to the genetic accident they have wrought. The stresses and strains within the home become our own and somehow shape us. As part and parcel of this package of fate comes, or develops, a personal capacity or incapacity to cope, survive, or even prosper. Some make it, and some don't. So much for theodicy.

A local fiddler whom I know, Seán, called to invite me to drive the long distance with him to Eoin's removal, spend the night, then attend the funeral and burial the next day. 'It's a rare day that you get to see a man laid out at home anymore. I thought that with your interest in Irish culture and appreciation of traditional music, you'd want to come along. The people of the area hang on to their traditions much longer than the rest of us do.

'Long before Eoin's body is in the ground your eyes will be rolling, your heart thumping, and tears flowing. Besides, every good musician within a hundred miles will be there for Eoin. There will be mighty tunes played and good craic for all.'

As we drove, Seán explained, 'Eoin's brother, I'm told, laid out Eoin in his bed at home yesterday. You see, Eoin's father is dead, and his eighty-six-year-old mother is in a nursing home. She lost her memory long ago, so his brother came back home to organise the funeral. This afternoon the coffin will have arrived, and they will have lifted Eoin into it. Eoin's family and friends are gathering at his home. This evening is the removal. The body will be carried to the church to lie in repose overnight, and the priest will bury Eoin tomorrow.

'In recent years rosaries are said in the funeral home rather than in the house, but a good number of the dead are still laid out in the house where they lived. That's the old-fashioned way. And it is one of the reasons I invited you to come along.

'Eoin was one of the finest musicians I ever knew, and could he write tunes! It was like part of his mind was hooked into choirs of angels who gave him inspiration. It was music that kept him alive so long. The music is what separated him from the black demon lurking in a corner of his soul that finally got him in the end.'

When we got to Eoin's house on a narrow, winding country road, there was a row of parked cars nearly a quarter of a mile long. We had no choice but to get out and walk. It was about seven in the evening and a dark mist had enveloped the area. Dozens of people were standing outside the front door of the house chatting with one another, often in Irish. The house looked like many others in the area, two storeys high, painted white, with patches of moss growing on the north wall and on the roof slates.

When we finally made our way to the living-room, there was Eoin, waxy pale, in a coffin resting on two plain wooden kitchen chairs. His brother was sitting at one end of a row of chairs placed close to the head end of the coffin. It was a newly made, old-fashioned looking, pine coffin that was shaped something like a mummy case. Other family members sat next to Eoin's brother. Nearly everyone in the room was talking quietly. I noticed, under the coffin, a basket full of hundreds of envelopes containing Mass cards that had been purchased by mourners. Each card entitled Eoin to a priest saying a Mass for him.

We stopped at the coffin, looked down at Eoin for a respectful moment, bowed our heads, then moved along to shake hands with each of the family members and to tell them that we were sorry for their troubles. Then we gradually made our way into the crowded, smoky kitchen where Eoin's teenaged cousins were pouring pint glasses of Guinness from a keg, or Paddy whiskey from a bottle into smaller glasses. They also served non-alcoholic drinks. There were some women standing there with eyes red from crying.

I asked Seán what the people who were speaking Irish were talking about. He said, 'Some are saying how sad they are that Eoin is gone. Others are telling stories about what a great musician he was, how he had great gifts. There were a few references to his depression.'

In what seemed like another twenty minutes, suddenly all

talking stopped and everyone crowded back towards the living-room. A priest began saying prayers. Although we couldn't see the priest, we could hear him. He was praying in English and led the mourners through a decade of the Rosary, after which Seán excused himself to go carry the coffin.

The procession to the church jerked me into a state of awe. Up front were Seán and five other musicians carrying the coffin on their shoulders. I saw them lift it not by the handles, but as if it were a box without handles. Each musician rested the bottom of the coffin on his shoulder, holding it with his outside hand, head and neck, with his inside hand resting on the outside shoulder of the man who was standing on the other side of the coffin. Eoin's brother, as well as other family members, were next in line. The priest had apparently driven on ahead to the church. Hundreds of friends and neighbours joined the proces-sion, most walking, and some driving their cars, following the mourners who were on foot. The long walk to the church took nearly half an hour; friends of Eoin's took turns in carrying the coffin. At first the parade seemed to me rather macabre. After several minutes of walking, though, I began to sense how really reverential it was. It was as if the soul of the community was embracing and honouring the soul of Eoin.

The grey-haired priest met the coffin at a side door of the church. Eoin's coffin was placed on a dolly, covered with a pall, sprinkled with holy water by the priest, and then rolled by the pallbearers following the priest up to lie in repose at the front of the church in the centre aisle close to the altar. The family fol-lowed along to seats reserved at the front of the church, while the other mourners found seats in the middle and rear of the church. As Eoin's procession was moving toward the altar the priest, reading from a liturgical text, intoned, 'May Christ free you from torments, deliver you from eternal death, claim you as one of his flock, and grant you a place among the elect.'

Just as the coffin was brought to rest at the front of the church, the priest said, 'May the prayers of Mary, the Mother of God, who stood by the cross as her Son was dying, help those who mourn for Eoin. May she give them the comfort of her own faith and by her prayers lead them on to the happiness of Heaven …' The priest then set down his book and addressed the family and mourners, giving them assurances that Eoin had lived his life in Christ. He announced that the funeral would be held in the church at 10 a.m. the next day, encouraged Eoin's friends to participate in a musical gathering at a local pub, said a few more prayers and concluded by leading the mourners in a hymn that he indicated was one of Eoin's favourites.

I left the church with the rest of the crowd and waited outside for Seán. He collected his fiddle and we went to the pub, which was as smoky and packed as Eoin's kitchen had been. Seán, Pádraig, a red-haired piper, a banjo player, an accordionist and bodhrán player were soon performing a number of Eoin's traditional music tunes and, as the evening wore on, many other old favourite jigs, hornpipes and reels were heard as well. The pub, which by law was to have closed much earlier, stayed open until about 2.30 a.m., serving porter, stout and whiskey. We finally got back to the B & B about 3 a.m.

As we entered the church the next morning for the 10 a.m. funeral Mass, the rain was slashing hard into the puddles outside. I sat in the last pew in an old Catholic church for the funeral of a man I never met, among a batch of three or four hundred parishioners, mourners and well-wishers. Seán sat at the front with the other pallbearers.

Death, I've noticed over the thirty summers spent in this unique land is a very big thing. Rural and small-town Irish often curse their neighbours behind their backs, but the moment the neighbour is dead, they say, 'God rest his soul; I've never had an unkind word to say about him.' Life-long enemy or not, they go to his funeral – sometimes, it seems, as a form of penance to avoid retribution for unkind words and deeds previously inflicted on the now dead man.

Unspoken, but apparently felt by the members of each community in rural Ireland is a concern – half-conscious, half-subliminal – that though the body may be dead, the ears, eyes, memory and soul are lurking close by and are probably able to detect even the most secret thoughts of anyone who approaches the coffin.

You call to the dead person's family, express condolences, send Mass cards. You go to where the body is laid out in repose, and you are seen to join in decades of the Rosary. Then you are also present for the removal of the body. You line up behind the coffin borne on the shoulders of six men, and you march to the church where the coffin is set down just in front of the altar. The Blessed Sacrament rests right behind the altar and spends the night close by the body and also with the still-lurking soul, helping it to prepare and qualify itself for the journey onward. The Pascal candle burns all night.

My friend, John Moriarty, an Irish poet and philosopher, once told me that the Pascal candle lighted at one's baptism is a wounded light and resurrection symbol. Each Pascal candle has five nails stuck in it, each representing one of Christ's wounds. So I thought of Eoin spending the night in his coffin at the church under the wounded light of the Pascal candle still burning at his funeral mass, heralding his resurrection.

Before the Mass, you shake hands with any family members standing at the door. You step inside, reach for the holy water and cross yourself with your wet finger tips. Facing the Blessed Sacrament and Pascal candle – just beyond the coffin – you genuflect before you enter the pew where you will be sitting. Or you proceed up the aisle and express your sympathies to the family members sitting in the first pew. If you are a close friend of the deceased, you bring a wreath of flowers and set it down on the floor beneath, or next to, the coffin and return to your pew, kneel down on the kneeler and pray for the dead person's soul and request divine comfort for the family.

You are certain to be on your very best behaviour and think only the purest of thoughts, because the dead man's soul may well know what is running through your mind, and God himself – present in the Blessed Sacrament – certainly does.

In every town in Ireland, for loved ones and dear friends you cry your heart out at their funeral and do everything you can to comfort the family. But at other funerals the dead person may be an old enemy or a person you didn't like very much, or perhaps more often a person you never knew well enough other than to call him by name. Still, you at least go to the funeral, if you haven't already been to the removal. Because if you don't, it will be noticed and things will be said about your not being there. A feud between families could be started by missing a neighbour's funeral. There is something inside you that expects most of these people to be at your own funeral. So you must pay your dues first.

I noticed a plaque on the wall – one of the twelve stations of the cross – labelled 'The Nailing'. Christ went through a lot of suffering, another reason to be reverent and still. This is no place for levity. When you're in the church with the coffin of the dead man and his family and the priest and all the other people, you certainly don't act the way you do in the pub having had ten pints of Guinness.

The priest, who was arranging things on the altar in his clerical black, stepped into the sacristy to put on his red cowl and vestments with the embroidered Alpha and Omega symbols and returned with the altar boy in tow. This grey-haired man had said thousands of funeral masses before. He knew how to do it.

Just before the Gospel reading, a woman who had been sitting up front next to Eoin's brother stepped up to the lectern. She sang some kind of lament in Irish – poignant, mournful, melodic. That brought on a little ache around my tear ducts. I learned later that the style of singing used in that lament is known as *sean-nós* (pronounced shan-nos), meaning old style. There have been many millions of Irish souls sent on their journey over the years by the sound of *sean-nós* songs.

The priest etched signs of the cross on his forehead, lips and breast and then read from the Gospel of John, the priestly prayer of Christ: 'Father, I want those you have given me to be with me where I am, so that they may always see the glory you have given me … so that the love with which you loved me may be in them, and so I may be in them.'

Then came the eulogising sermon, it was full of praise for Eoin. 'Such faith Eoin had,' said the priest, 'an example for us all, myself included.'

A strange feeling came over me. I felt that the priest was about to work some ritualistic magic in order to ensure Eoin's safe entry into Heaven. This hunch proved correct, as I later discovered, when reading the liturgical text entitled *Order of Christian Funerals approved for use in the Dioceses of Ireland*. The instructions to the priest at the beginning of the text stress that the Eucharistic sacrifice accomplishes a kind of purification of the deceased, implicitly necessary for admission through the Pearly Gates.

The moment after I had that premonition, the priest prayed over the gifts brought to the altar for the Eucharist: 'All-powerful and everlasting God, your Son offered himself to be our bread of life and poured out his blood to be our cup of salvation. Have mercy on your servant Eoin and let the Eucharist we offer be for him a help to salvation.'

After the Eucharist, the priest read the prayers for the soul of the dead making its journey to where it could be with Jesus on that great day of arising. He then took the holy water from the altar boy and shook it all over Eoin's coffin, saying that just as all sin was washed away at baptism, now with the shaking of this holy water, all remaining sin would be washed away, so Eoin could make his way unblemished into the Light: 'May the angels lead you to Paradise; may the martyrs come to welcome you.'

Then the priest stated that while he was removing his robes he would play a CD of uilleann pipe music. Returning in his clerical black suit, he again splashed holy water on the coffin.

Two young men removed the flowers, then assisted Seán and the other pallbearers in grasping the coffin to roll it down the aisle toward the church door. The red-eyed family followed.

The coffin was put in the hearse and the procession moved slowly through the village and turned left onto the road to the cemetery. All the shops in the town were closed. The rain had stopped and the low-lying dark grey clouds began to lift.

When the hearse arrived at the cemetery, Seán and the other pallbearers once again lifted the coffin up to their shoulders. The body of Eoin was the half-inch thickness of the coffin away from them, resting on their shoulders, snug also against their neck and cheek. There was a tenderness about them as they walked in a slow and fluid rhythm from the hearse to the grave that Seán said had been dug by two of his neighbours, which apparently is often still done.

At the graveside, after the priest's final prayers, the piper with curly red hair and beard, who had performed the night before at the pub, played Eoin's tune *pianissimo* as the mourners stood still, feeling the clutch in their throats.

Four men stretched two heavy, well-used hemp ropes around the coffin, one at the head, the other at the foot, and lowered Eoin's body down into the freshly dug hole in the ground. Then with their shovels they filled in the grave and placed upon the mound of earth the flowers that had been left in the church next to the coffin. The family and mourners stayed on for some time to talk with one another. A bottle of Irish whiskey was passed around from one mourner to the next. Each person would take a sip, then hand the bottle to another.

A friend of the dead man noted, 'Eoin often threatened suicide, saying, "The people won't appreciate me until I'm gone".' Another said, 'Not many, I'll tell you, are sent off this way, with sweet music, the priest making such a fuss over him, and so many people all feeling a powerful sadness in the air. What happened here today is a rare thing, indeed.'

Seán put his hand on my shoulder and said, 'They don't do it this way in America, now do they?'

'I'm afraid not.'

Seán rubbed his moustache and noted, 'A people that does not know how to honour its dead is a people without a soul'.

SOUL PORTRAITS

What kind of a soul does a people have who know how to bury its dead? Soul, construed singularly or collectively as the soul of a people, connotes a spiritual or moral essence. If it is a good soul, not only does it invest itself in an elaborate and poignant burial ritual but it is heart-centred in other ways as well.

A heart-centred soul is filled with empathy and compassion. It feels with intensity. These feelings predominate over detached analytical reasoning. The result is that heart usually prevails over cognition, passion over indifference. These proclivities are easily detectable in the form of feeling-filled speech the people employ. The Irish have a reputation for individually and collectively possessing such a soul.

The most all-encompassing single portrait of the Irish soul and character I have ever seen is about four hundred and thirty years old. It was first published in the third quarter of the sixteenth century by an Englishman. He was unlike a number of other English observers who tended to write books which castigated the Irish.

Its author, Edmund Campion, was an English Jesuit scholar who visited Dublin in 1570–1571, only to be executed ten years later as a traitor to England. Following his visit to Dublin, Campion wrote a book entitled *Histories of Ireland*. Campion had been educated at Oxford where he met Richard Stanihurst, who later settled in Dublin and became Speaker of the Irish Commons. Campion's characterisation of the Irish has been attributed to Stanihurst:

> The [Irish] people are thus inclined: religious, franke, amorous, ireful, sufferable of paines infinite, very glorious, many sorcerers, excellent horsemen, delighted with warres, great alms givers, passing in hospitalitie; the lewder sort (both clarkes [clerics] and laymen) are sensuall and loose above measure. They are sharpe witted, lovers of learning, capable of any study whereunto they bend themselves, constant in travaile, adventurous, intractable, kind hearted, secret in displeasure.[7]

While the expressions 'franke' and 'secret in displeasure' may seem to be contradictory, the word 'franke' in the sixteenth century meant free, i.e., not a slave or serf, also, free from restraint or impediment, unrestricted and unchecked. A twenty-first-century equivalent might be 'free spirit'.

Campion's list of Irish traits is most intriguing, despite its sweeping generalisations. Having read Campion's comments on the Irish I took each item on his list and compared them with my memories of over thirty years observing the Irish and I consulted with other judges of Irish character more capable than I.

I decided to start at the top of Campion's list where, you recall, he began with 'religious'. This is not an easy word to define, but some of its synonyms include: churchgoing, devotional, devout, divine, doctrinal, faithful, God-fearing, godly, holy, pious, pure, reverent, righteous, sacred, scrupulous, spiritual, unerring and unswerving.

As I reflected on these characteristics of being religious I began to suspect that I had never in my entire life met a person, in Ireland or anywhere else, who had managed to imprint upon his soul such an exhaustive and high-idealed set of virtues. Not even Ireland's plethora of ageing nuns, individually or collectively, would seem to measure up to such a high standard.

I decided that Campion must have had a slightly less rigorous frame of reference in mind when he chose to label the Irish as 'religious'. After all, he did note, 'that the lewder sort (both clarkes [clerics] and laymen) are sensuall and loose above measure'.

I remembered how, on each Sunday morning thirty years ago, virtually the entire able-bodied populace of Ireland went to Mass. The numbers of the faithful have declined considerably since then. But, compared to other western nations, the Irish do attend church with some commendable frequency. It is an open question, on a case by case basis, whether their doing so is motivated more by a fear of hell and divine retribution or by a saint-like desire to assimilate all of the virtues synonymous with being religious. There also remains a bit of community pressure to be seen at Mass.

Irish Catholic religiosity entails more than being seen at Mass and funerals, going to Novenas, or hosting 'stations' in one's house. The rural Irish have a disciplined propensity to cross themselves every time they pass – while walking or driving – a church, a graveyard, a grotto, a Marian roadside display, or a black spot (a road sign indicating a fatal accident). They also like to cross themselves whenever they, or someone else participating in the conversation, commits a blasphemy or even entertains a thought about performing an act which could possibly result in divine retribution.

'Franke', you recall, was Campion's second-listed Irish trait. As its meaning in Campion's time meant 'freedom loving', by implication, it would mean not loving anything that would constrain one's freedom such as, for example, laws or the authorities who created or enforced them. In fact, authority figures of any kind, especially English authority, would have been an anathema to Campion's Irish contemporaries. There is every reason to conclude that your modern day Irishman loves his freedom just as much. That is perhaps why Campion also listed the trait 'intractable,' meaning, difficult to influence or direct. The Irish have an eight-hundred-year reputation for resisting most constraints placed upon them by their conquerors or any one presuming to possess authority over them.

But 'frank' in the modern day sense of laying one's cards on the table and openly disclosing one's true feelings was not a feature of Irish character then, nor is it now. Campion's conclusions that the Irish are 'secret in displeasure' corroborates this. Being frank or direct in Ireland can be regarded as both naïve and rude. Between the era of the Norman conquest which began in 1169, and the Anglo-Irish Treaty of 1921, the Irish were a subjugated people. To speak the truth and dare to be frank about one's feelings under such circumstances could easily have meant death. No doubt, these many centuries of subjugation, often tyrannical, go a long way to explaining why the Irish normally eschew volunteering much in the way of information about their personal feelings. Instead of expressing themselves frankly or directly, many Irish prefer instead to intimate, or avoid the issue entirely. If you ask an Irishman, 'How have you been lately?' don't expect him to reveal very much.

As to the 'amorous' quality Campion detected, one would wonder if the Church's persistent preaching about the sins of the flesh might have substantially impeded Irish amorousness. Irish myths and legends featured tales of passionate amour. The Church, with all its threats of hell and damnation for falling prey to the sins of the flesh, must have intimidated many of the 'religious' Irish into foregoing sensual pleasures in order to achieve that heavenly reward. Yet despite those fifteen centuries of ecclesiastical implorations the Irish are no slouches when it comes to expressing their romantic feelings.

This does not mean that the only form of amorous activity in Ireland is coital. It does, however, remain the all-favourite form of expressing amorous feelings. Neither the damp, dark, climate of Ireland nor the influence of the One True Faith (with nearly 32 per cent of all Irish births being from unwed mothers) has in any way inhibited the Irish from competing fiercely with the Mediterranean cultures when it comes to acting 'amorously'.

'Ireful' is another trait of the Irish spied upon by Campion. Ireful suggests a range of emotions pertaining to dissatisfaction, discontent, irritation, and resentment at the milder end, to anger, fury, wrath and rage at the more heated extreme. Ire can arise out of simple frustration in achieving a task, totally unassociated with any wrongdoing on the part of another. It can be triggered by an injustice committed which did not directly affect the person, but was directed at another person or group of persons. It could be related to a begrudging or greed; insult, criticism, or abuse; being unfairly taken advantage of or otherwise having been victimised, cheated or stolen from, physically attacked, threatened or defeated. One of the Irish stereotypes is short-temperedness. 'Irish temper' is a well known expression conveying this trait.

Campion observed the Irish were 'secret in displeasure'. So how does one reconcile the apparent inconsistency? I've noticed that many Irishmen seem to have long fuses, but under sufficient and sustained provocation they tend to blow. The Irish tendency to contain ire and bear the insult may be why Campion wrote they are 'sufferers of paines infinite'. For a conquered people the choice is simple: suffer your pains silently or be further punished. Another dimension of suffering pain invokes saving a measure of face. Your average Irishman will let it brew inside himself until it becomes an obsession, but he'll never give the other person the satisfaction of seeing the pain. Campion's observation of 'constant in travaile', perhaps meaning weary from persistent hard knocks, may also stem from the many centuried subjugated status of the Irish people.

Present day ire is another question. Rural Irish society is a virtual fishbowl. Everyone is noticed and carefully observed by everyone else. Thus, people tend to work hard to maintain some semblance of a positive reputation in the community. Frequent displays of anger do not auger well for being looked up to by one's peers in the village. Therefore, some learn to suppress their anger. If they become excessive in their refusal to express bottled-up ire, it may fester into depression.

'Very glorious' perhaps is another way of saying glory seeking. Irish myths and legends are full of glory-seeking warriors. The most powerful ones became the king's champion. The champion sat at the king's right hand and was awarded the champion's portion of food. They boasted endlessly of their prowess. Warriors of ancient Ireland severed the heads of their slain enemies, tied them to their horses' manes for the journey home, and when they arrived home these heads were impaled on stakes in front of the warriors' lodge. Displaying a collection of the heads of one's slain enemies under almost any circumstances could be safely considered boasting or 'very glorious'. Thus, for Campion to add, 'delighted with warres' would seem to understate. 'The Pride of the Irish', a term recognised worldwide, stems from centuries of successful glory seeking.

Sitting in the clubhouse of an Irish football or hurling team before a match, listening to the athletes work themselves up into a battle frenzy, should leave no doubt that a good many of the present day warrior-type Irishmen are still 'delighted with warres'.

The terms 'many sorcerers' and 'excellent horsemen' tend to represent vocational skills perhaps more than soul quality. Sorcery is by no means a dead art in Ireland. But a capacity for working spells and conjuring spirits points to a certain species of soul quality just as much as being an excellent horseman testifies to an athletic bent. Ireland's ancient champions and their warrior companions and modern day horsemen in Ireland all show the trait characterised as 'adventurous'. Whether it has been plunging into battle, partaking of strong drink and feasting, or pursuing sultry women, the Irish have always been attracted to adventurous undertakings.

'Passing in hospitalitie' often involved combinations of all three of the above referred to 'adventurous' activities. 'Passing' as used by Campion to modify 'hospitalitie' probably meant 'surpassing in'. The Brehon laws, which governed the Irish for many centuries, mandated hospitality. Offering hospitality, when due, was not an option. Under the Brehon Law a base client was obliged to provide a feast for his lord and retinue during the winter. The duty of hospitality fell on all householders.[8] There were severe penalties for refusing it. So powerfully felt was this duty that a monastery from which guests were turned away lost its legal status and could be damaged or destroyed without compensation. The tradition of hospitality penetrates into the present. Irish weddings and funerals are highly elaborate affairs and often entail expenditure associated with providing hospitality, which would sometimes send the hosts to the bank to borrow money to cover the costs. Even the poorest of the Irish will offer you a cup of tea when you call at their home.

Making the effort to call at the home of another is to honour the person being visited. One normally brings a small gift when doing so. When dining one always brings flowers, wine or chocolates. The host responds with a multi-course dinner that could compare to the fare of a fine restaurant. If the guest compliments the hospitality, the host or hostess dismisses their six hours of preparing the feast as 'nothing, really nothing; it's barely a bite to eat'.

The institution of going to the pub is another example of

Irish hospitality. Nearly every local ecclesiastical event, including a routine Sunday Mass, is often followed by a good number of the parishioners heading for the pub. If one is bought a drink, one is expected to reciprocate.

We have already discovered what Campion characterised as the 'sharp-witted' Irish who, he told us, are also 'lovers of learning and capable of any study to which they lend themselves'.

That leaves us with two inter-related Irish virtues which Campion applauded. These are 'great alms givers' and 'kindhearted'. Perhaps because of, as well as in spite of, their subjugation the Irish have excelled at both. These twin traits were ingrained in the Irish personality long before St Patrick encouraged such virtues.

Nearly every tragedy reported in the Irish media, is responded to instantly by the Irish through their charitable contributions. A girl was born without arms or legs and needed constant medical attention to keep her alive. People all over the country sent money to the girl's parents. Publicans placed receptacles on the bar for contributions. The responses were identical to the news of young mothers being prematurely widowed by the untimely death of their husband, due to accident or murder.

Literally shiploads of their cattle have been sent to famine-stricken countries. The cows sent out are usually pregnant so that the donee will, in essence, receive two cows rather than just one. The instinctive Irish tendency to respond compassionately with the generous provision of alms sets an example for the world.

When on 11 September 2001 all flights to America were cancelled, Mary Sugrue, the chief management officer of Aer Rianta at Shannon airport organised for local families to take stranded airline passengers into their homes.

Just as the Irish characteristic 'ireful' is riddled with nuanced threads, so too is Irish 'kindheartedness'. As we have already discussed, both the generous giving of alms and the generous offering of hospitality constitute variations on a theme of kindheartedness.

Another one of these is showing mercy when the other fellow is down. I once knew a builder who was on the verge of bankruptcy. When his creditors learned of his plight, many of them looked the other way, rather than taking the builder to court. One of his creditors, a sub-contractor, was one of those who showed the builder some mercy. He stated, 'No sense kicking the man when he is down. The poor bastard is suffering enough'.

Another flavour of kindheartedness is that they are normally quick to forgive, particularly if the person who wronged them is repentant and apologises.

Other faces of Irish kindheartedness include graciousness and social cordiality. What has amazed me the most about this feature of the Irish demeanour is that local scoundrels are smiled at and greeted by name. What is said about them behind their back is another matter. It seems there are two standards about how one speaks about one's neighbours. One pertains to face to face and public statements which are most universally kind-hearted in content and tone. The other deals with what is said *sotto voce*.

The Irish still use the word 'salute' to mean a formal greeting associated with a gesture such as tipping one's cap. For many years the Irish would salute persons of some rank and stature, as well as their own friends, when passing them on the road. Today in many parts of rural Ireland many car drivers continue that tradition of saluting by raising the index finger from the steering wheel when meeting oncoming cars.

Kindheartedness in Ireland also entails helping others save face. Losing face is a serious matter for an Irishman. The Irish let each other get away with things in order to avoid causing another to lose face. You couldn't find a better source for explaining the importance of face than the legend of 'Bricriu's Feast'. This tale is about the champion's portion at a feast and how great warriors were willing to kill for it, or to die defending their right to it. For to have their rightful champion's portion denied them was to suffer the most agonising humiliation and scorn.

A male ego is more fragile and delicate than the last living pair of an endangered species. A woman could be divorced under the Brehon Law if she left her husband without cause. Even if she didn't leave him she could be divorced for bringing shame on his honour.

Irish women under the Brehon Law must have had sensitive egos as well and therefore were also in need of face-preserving legal mechanisms. An Irish wife could obtain a divorce if her husband repudiated her, spread a false story about her, or circulated a satire about her, or if she was tricked into marriage through sorcery. It was permissible to strike one's wife discreetly, but the husband dare not leave a bruise on her skin that would show.

To wrongfully lose one's honour, under the Brehon Law, was a litigatable offence and the wrongdoer was required to pay a heavy fine, then measured in cows or slave girls. The going price for a slave girl was, on average, three cows.

The closest forms of action under English Common Law related to 'face' are slander, defaming another by the spoken word; and libel, defamation in writing. To prevail, the plaintiff is required to prove that the defendant knowingly told a lie, with malice of intent. The plaintiff needs to prove actual, quantifiable economic injury. The only exception was slander or libel, *per se*, which meant that saying or writing certain things were presumed under the law to cause injury. Examples of what have been ruled slander *per se*, include calling a lawyer a 'shyster', or falsely alleging that someone has a 'loathsome disease'.

Under the Brehon Law, no economic harm had to be proved. Not only murder, wounding, or maiming or theft of valuables was compensated by an honour price which varied according to social rank. Also compensatory were satire and refusal of hospitality. The value of face in Ireland has survived to the present day.

My favourite contemporary story about the lengths an Irishman is willing to go in order to help another save face was told to me by a banker friend. An old woman returned home to Ireland having worked in America for years. She was highly dependent upon her social security cheque which would come in the post. If it were more than a day or so late in arriving she would tend to panic and fear starvation. Her cheque was mailed automatically to her house. So when it was late she would enlist the assistance of her bank manager. She would demand that he ring the American embassy in Dublin, which he dutifully did, but each time he would put his finger on the telephone button to prevent a connection from taking place. He would feign a conversation with the US ambassador and then inform the woman that the cheque would be delivered within the next seventy-two hours. The cheque was late on a number of occasions, yet the bank manager each time cheerfully pretended to ring Dublin.

Another good story involves a couple of neighbours. One man discovered that his next-door neighbour was sneaking over to his turf shed each night and stealing a basket of turf. So he placed a forty-two gallon metal drum up on his shed and braced it with a long pole onto which he tied a transparent fishing line.

He then fastened the other end of the line to a piece of turf on top of his turf pile. When the neighbour, the next evening, stopped by and grabbed the top piece of turf off the pile, the metal drum fell on his head, splitting his scalp wide open. The thieving neighbour ran back to his house and his wife ended up driving him to the hospital where his head was shaved, stitched and bandaged. The next day the two neighbours met outside their houses. The man whose turf had been stolen expressed great sympathy for whatever befell his bandaged neighbour, asking how he had injured himself. The neighbour responded that he had tripped over a stump in the field behind his house. Then they talked about the weather and wished each other a good day. This way no face was lost on either side.

Perhaps this principle was best explained by a neighbour who once remarked to me, 'You always put your best face on when you go out in public. When you come back to your house you can take it off.'

Any composite drawing of the Irish soul contains some seeds of truth even though it may depict features not entirely flattering of the subject. Proinsias MacCana, an Irish scholar as knowledge-able about ancient Irish character and values as he is about modern Irish stereotypes, stated that, '… primitive and unspoil-ed, crude and uncivilised, gifted but undisciplined, lyrical and romantic, dissembling and cunning, childish and wayward … None of these cliches, whether they have their origin in dis-interested observation or in ethnic or political prejudice is wholly without substance.'[9] Professor MacCana never asserted that the stereotypes he listed were wholly the truth. The stereotyped com-posite portrait contains only partial truth – certainly not partial truth that should be wholly ignored. But what is partial is incomplete.

Poetic truths contain symbols and metaphors, which suggest that 'A' (the object observed and commented upon) is like 'B' (the symbol or metaphor). National symbols tend to reflect the poetic unconscious of the people. The shamrock, a green, three-leafed plant, symbolises the Trinity. The Irish harp, an instrument known for its lyric voice, muse-like personality and mystical powers, is found on every euro coin minted in Ireland.

The shamrock and the harp are symbols which point, but do not limit or attempt to restrict. They each denote a self-transcending ideal. They also suggest a national bias for the arts, learning, the humanitarian and the spiritual. There are many other visual symbols of Ireland. These are often seen on picture calendars and postcards: Irish landscapes and cityscapes, castles and monasteries, farmers and fishermen, cows and sheep, stone walls and homesteads, sunshine and mist, music and dancing, drinking and storytelling, schoolchildren and scholars, footballers and hurlers, birds and wildflowers, fields and forests, painters and poets.

One of Ireland's contemporary poets, Seamus Heaney, in 1995 won the Nobel Prize for Literature. As a poet he uses symbols encoded in words. It is by the delicate crafting of language that the poet reaches the hearts of his readers. With his constellation of word symbols Heaney signals to us, 'At the level of poetic speech ... sound and meaning rise like a tide out of language to carry individual utterance away upon a current stronger and deeper than the individual could have anticipated.'[10]

In these character sketches, visual and biographical symbols have helped to paint a composite of the Irish soul. There are other aspects of this elusive soul which can be considered separately. How members of the rural Irish community regard one another is one of them. How they sometimes judge one another's character, and the values which underlie such judgements, can be quite revealing.

CATEGORICALLY SPEAKING

After fifteen years of coming to Ireland on holidays, I finally
mustered up the courage to purchase an Irish home, originally
built in 1844 as a school master's house. It overlooks beautiful
Kenmare Bay and the famous Macgillycuddy's Reeks, the tallest
mountains in Ireland. The house badly needed restoration.

I drew up detailed plans for how I wanted it restored and
found a builder to do the job. I naïvely thought it would be a
straightforward undertaking. What I didn't know at the time is
that the Irish Famine of the 1840s left a terrorising imprint on the
soul of every surviving Irishman. More than a million died and
another million fled the country to England, America, Canada
and Australia. That imprint was transmitted through generations and included most of the Irishmen alive in 1985, the year I
had bought the house. That subliminal fear of starvation had
given birth to a survival ploy known in Ireland as the 'long finger'.

The long finger meant that no matter how many construction jobs a builder had contracted for, they would never be
enough to cause him to feel secure. So he would start each new

job by working for a week or two. This would put his stamp on the job to ensure no other builder would seek to take it away from him. Then he would go find another job and work for a week or more before moving along to still another job. Only when the people threatened to sue would he stop procrastinating and return to any particular job.

Another builder's trick was that most of the work performed would be done by subcontractors who often did no more than show up at the job without any clear instructions from the absent builder regarding the work they were to perform. When they came I'd show them the plans and give them directions on what I wanted done. Whenever I asked, 'Can you handle that?' they would inevitably respond, 'I will, of course.' However, they usually did whatever they wanted and paid little or no attention to my requests.

One rare day when the builder showed up, I asked him, 'When someone in Ireland says, "I will of course", what does that mean?' The builder looked at me sympathetically and said, 'It means nothing at all. It's what you say when you want to make a fellow feel good.' It took me another two or three years to realise that in Ireland when confronted with a choice between being kind and telling the truth, an Irishman will often opt for being kind.

Noel O'Donoghue, a discalced Carmelite monk I met during research I was doing on St Patrick, explained this peculiar Irish trait. He said, 'The Irish will always tell you what you want to hear. So when you ask "Would you handle this or that?" they will normally say, "I will of course". That doesn't mean they intend to do it. If they know you want a "yes" answer, they will readily oblige you. There are many reasons for this. One is the Irish are indeed kindhearted and polite. Another is that as a subjugated people over so many centuries they said what they thought a person wanted to hear as a matter of self-protection. When, for example, dealing with their English oppressors the only way to survive was to make agreeable statements.'

It is one thing to understand this Irish trait as a matter of theory. It is another to modify one's own behaviour accordingly. I had to learn the hard way. One day, Sarah, and I were driving in a part of rural Ireland we had never previously visited. We knew where we wanted to end up. But we were not certain which way to turn. I thought we should take the left fork and Sarah thought it was the right. There happened to be a farmer standing at the side of the road. Full of confidence I held the map out the window and said, 'In order to get to such and such a town we need to take the left fork here, don't we?' He looked at me and announced, 'You do indeed'.

A half an hour later we asked for directions again. Instead of telling the person what I thought, I asked what he would advise. We followed his directions and got there. Then we looked at the map and realised that the farmer should have said 'Take the right fork'. But that would have caused me to lose face, so he agreed with my idea of how to get there, even though it was wrong.

Notwithstanding the fact that I had learned this lesson, I had not yet satisfactorily come to understand the psycho-dynamics of what underlies 'I will of course'. It wasn't until I met Brendan McHale, a wise and friendly priest, that I was able to unravel this enigma. Brendan explained that 'a person's intent is to make the individual he is talking to feel good. He also intends to do what he promises.

'But in practice here is what happens. The promise, "I will of course", is made in response to a request. The individual making the request seldom holds the promiser accountable for his commitment. Therefore, there is no loss of face for the person who fails to perform and therefore no inducement to perform.

'Thus, what often happens between the commitment and the time the promise is due, is that the promiser forgets what he said. Since there is no punishment for not performing, the promise never acquires an urgent status.'

Back at the building site, I remained perplexed about how more effectively to recruit the assistance I needed.

During the course of the slow and tedious work on the house, I befriended a local stonemason, Denis Casey, the same man who taught me about nature. He also taught me how to build stone walls and how to select a stone with a good face and artistically place it in the wall.

More importantly, he also taught me about Irish culture. Denis told me that few authority figures are liked in Ireland, including the boss on a job. Giving out orders would ensure the job would never get done. For eight hundred years the Norman and English conquerors of Ireland had given out orders, and no Irishman ever liked being told what to do. Nearly every rural family in Ireland can tell you stories about how their ancestors were unfairly treated by English landlords and their agents.

He told me to play the dumb, helpless Yank. 'Go to the man whose help you need, look worried, and ask if he could spare a moment to explain how to do the job. If you say that, he'll likely do the job himself. He will be the one coming to the rescue of a poor, ignorant Yank, and that will make him happy.'

I did what Denis instructed and the results were miraculous. In Ireland a humble request is far more powerful than a direct command.

Listening to the men talk while working on my house taught me a number of things. One is how people evaluated one another in our community. The first subdivision consisted of 'us' and 'them'. 'Us' meant the people born and raised in the town. 'Them' meant Protestants, foreigners, blow-ins, outsiders, travellers (sometimes called gypsies, tinkers or itinerants), hippies, and, more recently, asylum seekers.

According to Denis 'a foreigner comes from any other country. A blow-in is basically the same as an outsider. It's someone from elsewhere in Ireland. To be considered a blow-in or outsider you just have to come from as far away as the next town over. If you were a local man and you married a wife from the village of Kilgarvan, seven miles down the road from here, and you brought her back here to live with you, she'd be known as an outsider or blow-in. She might as well have come from Dublin. Her children wouldn't be looked at the same as if they were children born of local families.'

Outsiders and blow-ins who have lived in the same small town for thirty or forty years are still regarded as 'not one of us'. A group who are members of the local golf club, stage a 'Blow-in Golf Tournament' every year. As a not so subtle joke, they established a rule that a blow-in must have lived in the town for at least twenty-five years before he's eligible to participate.

Another classic case of 'not one of us' involved two elderly gentlemen, one aged ninety-three, the other ninety-one, who are from a small village not too far away. At least once a week after several pints of Guinness they got into an argument as to who is the oldest man in the village. The ninety-one-year-old claims that he is the oldest man in the village. His rationale was that the ninety-three-year-old was born on a farm a couple of hundred yards outside the village.

Denis continued, 'as for the travellers, or "tinkers", the British landlords would evict a young woman and her children if her husband died. The landlord would toss the family off if there was any trouble from the tenant. They were left on the road with no place to sleep or live. So they just wandered about from place to place and ended up doing odd jobs like sharpening knives or axes. They lived in wagons pulled by a horse and they often had to steal to keep from starving. So all the people you see today living in caravans along the side of the road are travellers or tinkers. They didn't come from Hungary as gypsies the way some people think. No, that's wrong altogether. Each of the tinkers you see in the caravans has ancestors who were put off estates by the British landlords.'

'Tinker', in recent years, has become a pejorative term, and 'traveller' has become its politically correct replacement.

'"Hippies" are usually from England,' Denis explained. 'They started coming over in the 1960s. They have long hair, rarely take a bath, wear weird clothes and Doc Marten boots, hardly worked a day in their life, smoke pot and believe in free love.'

The latest foreign threat is the asylum seekers. These are persons who claim to be political refugees and slip into Ireland undetected, then assert political refugee status whether or not their lives are, in fact, in danger should they return to their home country. Many are from the former Soviet Union or Warsaw Pact countries, Yugoslavians, and Africans from countries that are in the midst of civil wars or ravaged by famine.

These asylum seekers have been entering the country in large numbers in recent years years. They are protected under European Union law from deportation until their case is properly heard. Many have been unable to prove their lives are in danger due to their political affiliations and beliefs.

The response of the Irish public is mixed: a lot of fear and some compassion. The fear usually consists of concern about their spreading disease, plus the fear of their stealing, begging and driving down property values and scaring away tourists.

While restoring the house, I was also preparing papers to present at the annual meeting of the Irish Medieval Society. Some of the issues I was researching were: who were the lawyers and judges St Patrick made reference to in his *Confession*; what kind of law were they practising; how were they able to be of assistance to St Patrick, who himself was a foreigner from Roman Britain; and how were the lawyers and judges related to the druids?

I began to suspect that the societal values evident in the ancient Brehon Laws, which were contained in manuscripts from the seventh and eighth centuries through the fourteenth to sixteenth centuries, might have percolated down further through the subsequent centuries so as to impose their influence on present day society. Names, language, literature, music, dance, major seasonal holidays, and gene pool have survived for aeons – it is not entirely beyond belief that some core societal values might have survived as well.

During the period covered by the Brehon Laws, the predominantly agricultural economy was a self-sufficient mixed farming arrangement involving cattle, sheep and pigs and the growing of cereal grains.[11] This economy was sustained by the inter-relationship of lord and tenant. The lord advanced the stock or land and the tenant paid the lord rent and services. This system produced enough wealth to support not only a hierarchy of lords and kings but also a professional class which included poets, judges, smiths and physicians. In pre-Christian Ireland most of these, except for the craftsmen, would be of the druid class.

The establishment of the Church gradually diminished the influence of the druids as such, but their vocational responsibilities related to poetry, genealogy, history, law and medicine continued. The Church, after some time, took over the religious function of the druids.

Society was hierarchical, tribal and rural in which the family unit, rather than the individual, assumed greater importance. The name of a tribe or people was *tuath* (pronounced too-ah). These *tuatha*, clans or more literally people, of which approximately one hundred and fifty once existed, were each ruled over by a petty king or underking, known as a *rí*. These petty kings owed allegiances to higher ranking kings known as *rí tuath*, or overkings. The laws each *tuath* adopted were similar to one another, as the jurisprudential custom and usage of the overall society had probably endured by trial and error before taking the form of legislation. But what appears to me as one of the most remarkable features of this system of laws was that, unless a treaty had been negotiated with a neighbouring *tuath* which provided for reciprocal protection of the people of the two *tuatha*, any person except clergy, lawyers or judges and poets who crossed over the boundary of his *tuath* into a neighbouring *tuath* was fair game to be killed. He had virtually no rights. For all practical purposes, the person living on the other side of the mountain or river in another *tuath* was treated essentially the same as a person from another country.

Under Brehon Law tracts a person with legal standing within his own *tuath* was called an *aurrad*, and the person from the other side of the mountain or river in another *tuath* was called *deorad*, or outsider. When the outsider, not protected by a treaty, entered another *tuath* he was known as *ambue*, a person without rights, and he could be killed or injured with impunity. This particular Brehon Law arrangement was not entirely irrational. Over the aeons people from other *tuatha* of the warrior class would come charging into a neighbouring *tuath* to wage wars, steal cattle and slaves, even commit arson or murder, rape and plunder.

Such *ambue* were either *deorad* or *cúglas*, an exile from overseas or literally, grey dog. Both could be killed at will. It was only some time after St Patrick had brought Christianity to Ireland that foreign priests were given the same protection to travel freely from *tuath* to *tuath* as was conferred upon the native Irish learned class. Hence, Patrick, who had once been a foreign slave in Ireland, had no more rights upon his subsequent arrival as bishop in Ireland than he would have had earlier as a slave. The lawyer judges, who helped him at the request of the king who chose to afford him protection, would have negotiated protection for him by treaty with neighbouring *tuatha*.

This sense of 'us' and 'them' was so strongly ingrained in Irish consciousness that until the reign of Brian Boru, who died in 1014, no provincial king in the history of Ireland was able to muster the support of the entire island and thus become the high king of all of Ireland. That such a feat was even possible then was due to two major factors: the Vikings had been successfully raiding and invading Ireland with near impunity for an entire century, and Brian Boru, king of Munster, had the vision, cunning and strength of character to persuade the other provincial kings that without a coordinated approach under central leadership, the Vikings would continue to devastate the whole of Ireland at will.

Ironically, in the Battle of Clontarf, high king Brian Boru's forces finally defeated the Vikings, but after the battle had concluded, a solitary Viking entered the ageing Boru's tent and slew him. Following the victory at Clontarf no successor to Boru was able to attain the support of all of the provincial kings and reign unchallenged as the high king of Ireland.

The maxim 'He who is not one of us is not to be trusted' still constitutes a major warp thread of Irish consciousness. But 'he who is one of us' is not automatically trusted.

There are so many ways in Ireland to construct 'them' and 'us' bifurcations that a comprehensive list could consume reams. As a general principle, the more local the group, the stronger the bonds. A local identity is usually far stronger than a national identity. Nearly every town or village in rural Ireland is so full of local pride that its people tend to think it is the best there is in all of Ireland.

But the smaller the better. The gradation runs as follows from the most to the least highly localised: subdenomination of a townland; townland; parish; town or village; county; province and nation.

But there are other important categories. Nearly all the rural people of Ireland dislike Dubliners. They call them individually Dub or *Jaicín*, pronounced Jackeen, which means a Dublin city slicker. In contempt for rural Ireland's perceived lack of high-cultured, urbane sophistication, Dubliners refer to the rural Irish as 'Culchies', implying a near total lack of cultural sophistication. The term appears to have originally been taken from Cuilche Mách, a town in County Mayo.

Then there are people who prefer to speak Irish as their first language. They usually live in the Gaeltacht, enclaves of Irish-speaking persons concentrated in various parts of rural Ireland. These people maintain not only the Irish language, but also its more traditional customs. Other Irish speakers use the language as a matter of national pride and are often in the academic profession. The Irish speakers believe that the 'rat race consumer-ised culture' is killing the country.

The 'us–them' categorisations that I find the most fascinat-ing are highly localised. They fall into two distinct types: those which evaluate individuals according to a combination of their moral character, competence and reliability; and those which evaluate persons according to the amount of authority they seem to possess. The less a person's moral character, competence and reliability, the less a person is trusted. The more authority a person has and flaunts, the less that person is liked.

Before delving into some examples, it is useful to recall the instance of how a person from another *tuath* was nearly always negatively regarded. When a class of people is disliked no one wants to imitate them. The result is often that local manners, customs and behaviours are adhered to, which positively re-inforces them. Patterning one's behaviour after the enemy or 'them' is avoided. Such positively reinforced localisation of valu-es over the centuries has had the effect of producing a vocabu-lary which features many expressions unique to each particular area. This is especially true of Irish slang expressions which often vary considerably from place to place in Ireland.

Hence, some of the expressions I will be employing to des-cribe another's moral character, competence or reliability – or lack of it – while common in the area of Ireland with which I am the most familiar, may not be used in other parts of the country. Or if such expressions are used, they may have slightly different meanings. Regardless, each locality has its own combination of terms it uses to label the reputation of its various inhabitants.

As has been the case with nearly all other aspects of my on-the-scene education regarding various unique features of the Irish culture, I have been privileged to sit at the feet of a number of perspicacious Irish tutors. My grasping the meaning of Kerry terminology was derived primarily from a man named Dinny whom I met at Listowel Writer's Week, May 1999.

From working on my house and overhearing the workers' comments on the reputations of various local individuals, I had assembled a bit of local slang expressions, often pejoratively employed, and I sought definitional assistance from a number of reliable sources. But no one could hold a candle to Dinny's in-cisive perceptions.

He explained that there are only three positive terms of reference within the group of locals referred to as 'us'. These include 'gentleman', 'sound man' and 'gas man'. Many Irish tend to feel that it requires death to acquire gentleman status. At funerals, one often nods one's head in sadness and comments, 'He was a fine gentleman'. My experience is that out of Irish kind-heartedness, many persons so described would not have earned that highest of accolades were they still alive. To be alive and referred to face to face as a gentleman usually means the person paying the compliment either hopes to procure a favour, or he has just succeeded in doing so. But to refer publicly to another man as a gentleman, who is not present at the moment the term is used, is the highest compliment possible.

Ranking merely half a notch below gentleman is the sound man. This means a man of sound mind and sound judgement who is also highly competent and reliable.

A gas man could be either a gentleman or a sound man. But he could also be morally corrupt, or an alcoholic or totally incompetent and never reliable. To earn gas man status one merely has to be a witty raconteur, full of jokes and stories and always entertaining and fun to be around.

We next consider those categories of persons who are perceived to be some combination of morally corrupt, incompetent or unreliable. I was surprised to discover that there are far more derogatory, than complimentary, terms employed in rural Ireland. Some of the terms and nearly all of the definitions are predominantly the reflection of Dinny's observational skills.

A *cute hoor* – a man so smart he can convince you to buy what you don't need so that he can borrow it. Hoor is the Irish way of spelling the other word normally preceded by a 'W'. This, in essence connotes the same level of moral sensitivity. This term is sometimes used in admiration of a person who manages to beat the system. But it is also used with disdain for someone who overcharges you or otherwise cheated you out of some money.

A *galvanised hoor* – despite being less clever than the cute hoor, he is actually worse as he will outlast him.

A *waster* – someone who will break his back to avoid work; he will actually spend more effort avoiding it than it would take to get it done.

A *knacker* – someone who takes something of value from you by any means available to him, such as outright theft, fraud, or deception. The term was originally applied to crooked horse traders and the purchasers of dead animals.

A *chancer* – someone who believes that effort and experience are the same thing. Even with no training at all, he thinks if he tries hard enough he will know how to do it. He expects to be hired despite his total lack of skills.

A *blackguard* – a person who was born without a conscience and never acquired one. If you gave him the shirt off your back he would come back for the braces.

A *gombeen man* – will help you get a price for your cattle that won't offend the buyer, and is otherwise usurious. He works through his connections and appears servile but is two-faced and self-serving.

A *bastard* – someone so cruel he will set you alight just so he can refuse to put you out.

A *begrudger* – someone who resents you because you didn't fail as well as he did.

A *bollix* – someone who fouls up everything he touches. His incompetence is not motivated by crooked dealings, but rather by stupidity, ignorance and indifference to excellence in any form.

A *wanker* – someone who is a hybrid of a bollix and a bastard.

There is a little of each of these qualities in nearly every one, according to Dinny, and it is a rare person indeed who perfectly exemplifies any one quality. Also many of these definitions depend on your point of view, for example to the English, Daniel O'Connell was a perfect cute hoor. He once got a man off for cattle thieving on the grounds that the animal was already dead, thus the man only stole the beef. Yet to many Irish people he remains to this day a shining example of a sainted gentleman. However, there are signs that one can look for and be wary of. Some of these signs are obvious, others less so. But only the foolhardy ignore them, especially if more than one sign of incompetence, unreliability or corruptness is exhibited by a single person.

There are so many derogatory terms with only the categories of gentleman, sound man and gas man to offset them. Some say this is the result of instinctive Irish suspicion and distrust, while others suggest such categories flow from a healthy scepticism, based upon experience.

The female equivalent of the gentleman is a good woman or a lady. A female who is regarded as the opposite of this category is referred to as a bitch. If she has the reputation of being absolutely incorrigible, she is referred to as a lighting bitch.

Having considered the most common forms of 'not one of us', therefore 'one of them' and the derogatory and complimentary categories of 'us', we now return to where we began: authority, a quality and power to which few Irishmen in the history of the country ever enjoyed submitting themselves. In Ireland all you need to do is choose certain professions that carry the badge of authority, and you will be disliked and distrusted, even though to your face people may act as if they are treating you with respect.

Nearly every authority figure of any kind is disliked in Ireland. Most authority figures enjoy some measure of status, and status is resented because either historically people with status maltreated other people or people without status begrudged those who had it. People with authority or status tend to rub others the wrong way, and they therefore set themselves up as targets of ridicule and scorn. Accordingly, it is quite common for your average Irishman not only to dislike – and only begrudgingly respect – authority and status figures. But also they take great delight in defying, sabotaging and tricking such persons. Furthermore, if the status is undeserved, people delight in contributing to their downfall.

The guards are underappreciated public servants entrusted with enforcing the law. One of the least popular laws used to require closing the pubs no later than 11.30 p.m. Often the publican would announce the last round of drinks and say that the pub is closing. A number of the people leave but the serious drinkers linger while the publican pulls down the shades, and switches off the outside lights. He then locks the front door and continues serving drinks.

Under the law, guards must not be stationed in their hometown. That makes them automatic outsiders, as well as authority figures. That is two bad qualities in one.

I heard a story involving a guard sergeant, out of uniform, drinking after-hours in a local pub along with at least fifty other locals. Two guards from the neighbouring town had arrived about 2 a.m. to conduct a raid. When they recognised the sergeant, they had a private talk with him, then soon left. The sergeant reported that the raiding guards said they received a call from a woman reporting that she heard her husband was being beaten up at the pub. But the locals said that was a cover story as the guards couldn't arrest the after-hours drinkers and let the sergeant completely off the hook.

One fellow who was a local footballer, went off to train for the guards. When he came back into town for a short visit proudly wearing his new guard's uniform, his former friends would not speak to him. He was no longer 'one of us'. He had become 'one of them'.

Not only do the guards enforce the no after-hours drinking laws, they also enforce the laws against bootleg booze, known in Ireland as poteen (*poitín*). The farmers who make poteen (not unlike vodka) from potatoes in their stills are always wary of being raided by the guards. Their faithful customers, who buy poteen at less than half the price of licensed whiskey, often go out of their way to protect their source of this particular libation.

One day a man overheard two guards talking at a pub about how the next morning they were going to raid a certain farmer's house, as he was reputed to be a big supplier of poteen. The man rang the farmer and told him to expect a raid at about 10 a.m. The farmer knew that the guard involved had a heart condition and that a good fright might stir the fellow up a bit. The farmer also knew that the guard himself was a mighty man for the drink and was often overheard saying that he drank because of his heart condition.

So the farmer left his huge bull loose outside his front door and kept the gate closed which led to his adjoining pasture full of cows, which the bull took great pride in servicing.

When the guard came the next morning, the farmer told him to watch out because his 'mad bull' was on the loose and he normally charged strangers.

'What should I do?' asked the guard. The farmer told him to run as fast as he could to the gate, open it and run into the next pasture where he'd be safe for sure.

The guard did as he was told and when the bull saw that the gate separating him from all those beautiful cows was about to be opened, he chased the guard who was so frightened that he climbed up a tree and nearly had a heart attack in the process.

Soon the bull was happily mingling with the cows. The farmer walked over to the tree to help the guard down, who was still trembling in fear. 'How do you feel?' asked the farmer.

'I've had a fierce desperate fright and a drink would do me no harm.'

'Come with me,' said the farmer, 'and we'll set you straight in no time.'

The farmer took the guard into his kitchen and poured him a half glass of poteen.

After the guard had a good swallow, the farmer handed him the just opened jug of poteen and said, 'Take the bottle for yourself and say nothing about the mad bull.'

With that, the farmer had outfoxed the guard who, having drunk the poteen, could do nothing to hurt the farmer.

Just as poteen makers and after-hours drinkers dislike obeying the law, so do car owners on some of the inhabited islands off the Irish coast. They refuse to tax and insure their cars, or have them inspected and as a result of such persistent and longstanding refusals the government now exempt them from any such responsibility by simply declining to enforce the law.

I am never offended by any of this *craic* as it seems to fit the anti-authoritarian demeanour of the Irish people. At times it can be downright amusing. I'll be walking along one of these island roads and all of a sudden I'll hear a roar behind me that sounds like a tank. I turn around quickly to discover a ten-year-old boy driving a car with no muffler, doors or windshield. I jump off the road, expecting that the vehicle also lacks brakes.

The bailiff stories are like legends of ancient Irish heroes. Bailiffs have the responsibility for protecting salmon and deer and preventing anyone from taking them out of season, improperly, or without a licence. The schemes the local poachers concoct to outwit the bailiffs are nearly endless. Tricking a bailiff in some novel way is often regarded as an act of creative brilliance.

Nearly every politician – from county councillors to TDs (members of the Irish Parliament, known as the Dáil) – is regarded as a cute hoor or he wouldn't have run for office in the first place. Most Irish expect their politicians to be corrupt as they believe that is the way the system works. So that is why some people are quick to befriend the local politician as he is the one who can produce government subsidies, free medical cards, special government payments and other tangible benefits.

But county council officials are often detested. They have the right to grant or refuse planning permission to build a house, garage, shed or extension. They can also impose costly and restrictive conditions. I've known Irishmen in remote areas, far from the county seat, to refuse to apply for planning permission and just build without it. Sometimes they succeed and other times the county planning authority requires them to knock down the building. Some complete about 90 per cent of the work and then apply for retention.

Priests have for several centuries been men of great power and influence. Sometimes the exercise of such power engenders the reaction, 'Who does he think he is, telling us what to do?' This effect is compounded if the priest holds himself out as speaking with the direct authority of God. Suspicion is definitely aroused. Words like 'hoor' or 'hypocrite' may be spoken behind his back.

Because of the countless number of sex scandals, respect for clergy has plummeted. It has also fallen from other abuses of power over the years. One of the most critical indictments of the Church I heard was uttered by a former nun. She said, 'Years before we were getting close to shaking off the English yoke, the Church had already decided it would be taking over next and make us its slaves.' Most of the priests who are respected have worked long and hard to earn it.

Teachers in Ireland, until the early 1980s, could hit their students. They had acquired a university education, so status and respect was therefore begrudgingly accorded them. They still have a powerful influence on their students. Hence, dependence, fear and hatred are sometimes intertwined in the way students feel about their teachers. Nevertheless, students love to tell stories about how they drive their teachers mad. Whenever a teacher leaves a classroom unattended, if even for a few moments, there is a very good chance that the students will be making a racket.

Doctors have the power of life and death, and are often some of the wealthiest members of the community. They are well educated and there is much status that comes with being a doctor. In days long ago the price of a visit to a doctor for a low wage earner seemed almost too steep to be worth paying. So the doctor was to be avoided if at all possible. People don't take kindly to a man whose training enables him to determine whether one is going to live or die. How does he know? What is there to assure me that the tablets he prescribes will cure my illness, rather than make it worse? Why should he profit from an illness that is no fault of my own?

My favourite 'distrust the doctor' story involved a widow who reluctantly went to the doctor. She mashed two of her tablets into powder and mixed it with the milk and bread to feed her chickens. When the chickens were alive the next morning she decided she could risk taking the tablets herself.

Solicitors, I can say from experience (being a lawyer myself), tend toward acting somewhat aggressively and are sometimes known for their arrogance. Some solicitors are also cute hoors. Your average Irishman will regard a solicitor with respect on one hand while harboring resentment on the other.

With apparent ironic pride one solicitor has a painting on his office wall of two farmers fighting over a cow. One is holding the head while the other is grasping the hind-quarters. A solicitor is depicted in the middle, calmly milking the cow.

In Ireland solicitors are regarded as legitimate terrorists, as the letters they write on behalf of their clients often strike terror in the hearts of the persons receiving them. When rural Irish people tire of asking for money owed them or have some other legal complaint, they go to their solicitor and ask him to write a letter to the offending person. Fearing a court fight, the debtor often pays his debt or takes action to avoid further controversy.

Judges are also fair game for being attacked by the freedom-loving and authority-despising Irish. One manner in which the Irish government deals with its various scandals is to establish a special tribunal, an evidence-gathering operation presided over by a Supreme Court Justice who has the authority to call witnesses from both the government and private sector. One such tribunal, named after the justice who presided over it, is the Flood Tribunal. Since 1999 it has been investigating allegations that County Dublin planning officials had been bought off by large building contractors. The money allegedly paid to the planning officials would result in their issuing planning permission for controversial projects. One witness called was a man in his seventies who had worked for a large building contractor and who had allegedly been instrumental in persuading County Dublin planning officials to issue planning permissions for projects important to his boss. His name is James Gogarty.

Who would think that a man under suspicion of multitudinous wrongdoing could be given positive treatment in the Irish media? One radio show host was so taken with Mr Gogarty's attitude that he had a transcript made of Gogarty's testimony before the tribunal and hired actors to read the transcript over the radio. This was because live broadcast of the actual Flood Tribunal was not permitted. Gogarty became so loved by the Irish public that pensioners rode the train from all over the country to Dublin each day to watch him perform in the tribunal.

What did Mr Gogarty do to achieve such instant national acclaim? He talked down to solicitors and to Mr Justice Flood. He criticised and ridiculed these powerful figures and, by his wit and charm, got away with it. He took on the legal and judicial establishments and made them look like they weren't as smart as they thought.

Another story of a judge from a lower court – known as the District Court – bears repeating. Judge Ó hUaidgh – a legend in his own time – was accustomed to dealing with prostitutes, petty thieves and other common criminals.

One day a young guard who had just graduated from Templemore, the national police training academy in County Tipperary, was called as a witness in a case in which the guard had charged a man with vagrancy. The alleged crime had occurred at the top of Westmoreland Street in Dublin.

Judge Ó hUaidgh asked the young guard to present the facts of the case. The guard said, 'When I told the accused to move on, he told me to feck off.'

Judge Ó hUaidgh responded, 'Tell me guard, why didn't you? Case dismissed'.

One day the same judge was trying a number of criminal cases against prostitutes. In the middle of the proceedings a group of young women law students entered the court room on an official tour as part of their legal training. Distracted by the noise they made and suspecting they were affiliates of the accused, Judge Ó hUaidgh barked at them: 'Sit over there with the other prostitutes. Move quickly. We don't have all day to waste'.

Accountants are disliked because they learn all about one's financial secrets. One accountant told me that the most common fear of her clients is that she will inform the government about their financial secrets.

We come now to the tax man. England for centuries taxed the Irish largely by customs and excise duties; and English landlords extracted fortunes from their poor Irish tenants. When Ireland became independent in 1921, the Irish transferred their distrust of British taxation officials to the new Revenue Commissioners. Evading payment of taxes in Ireland is known as tax fiddling. A 1983 European Union-sponsored survey found that the Irish are not exceptionally honest, by European standards, in matters of civic honesty. On tolerating tax fiddling they come out on top. Over a third of the Irish polled justified tax fiddling compared with only a quarter of Europeans as a whole.

Several years ago the Revenue Commissioners, realising that billions of pounds of taxes were outstanding, declared an amnesty that would allow delinquent tax payers to pay their long over-due taxes without interest if they paid their back taxes by a date certain. After the deadline the delinquent taxpayer would be charged for taxes, plus interest, and the Revenue Commissioners would seize the assets from the taxpayers' accounts. The name, address and amount of money seized from each delinquent taxpayer was published in the *Irish Times*.

I noticed that the man with whom I had a 10 a.m. appointment that day, had four hundred and fifty thousand pounds seized from his account by the Revenue Commissioners. As I sat in the waiting-room within easy earshot of his desk, I overheard one of his friends commiserating with him. His sympathetic friend said, 'I know how you must feel. The bastards took your own money from you. No trial at all. It was unfair. The blackguards have no right to it. You worked hard for every pound you earned. It belongs to you, not them. It's sheer robbery. The country has gone to Hell. The government now believes it has the right to rob its own citizens. There's no fairness in it. It's a crime what they did to you.'

I'm told that with the current rise in Irish prosperity people are more willing to pay taxes. Besides, with computers, the Tax Commissioners can catch you quicker, they say.

As a seasoned and wise solicitor once explained to me, 'There's no disgrace in Ireland for not paying taxes. The only disgrace is in getting caught'. He also summarised Irish attitudes in general toward obeying the law: 'Laws were made to be broken. We break the rules as often as we can, and, when we can't break them, we bend them instead.'

Irish ingenuity in rule bending is nearly peerless worldwide. An acquaintance I have made from Ballincollig, just west of Cork city, explained to me that until recently, under the Gaelic Athletic Association (GAA) rules, no GAA athlete was permitted to participate in a non-GAA sporting event such as rugby or soccer. A famous Cork GAA hurler wanted to attend a soccer match to root for the Cork team. His GAA hurling manager told him that it wouldn't look good having a prominent hurling star such as himself attending a non-GAA match. 'Entirely against the rules,' the hurling manager said. But realising there would be no stopping his man from going to the soccer match, the manager said, 'I'll appoint you to the vigilante committee so you can be on the lookout for GAA men who might be breaking the rules by attending the same soccer match as yourself.'

In the mind of your categorically speaking Irishman, once you brush aside the foreigners, outsiders, blow-ins, Protestants, travellers, hippies, asylum seekers, cute hoors, wasters, knackers, chancers, blackguards, gombeen men, bastards, begrudgers, bollixes, wankers, bailiffs, bossmen, guards, politicians, priests, teachers, doctors, solicitors, accountants, tax men and bitches, there is only a small handful of gentlemen and kind women left.

And don't you try to force me to commit myself on this matter. Now, as for yourself, I'm not so sure. But even if you fit into one or more of the above-listed categories of undesirable people, and yet you have proved yourself a gas man, I'll generally buy you a drink, especially after-hours. Then we can converse, which is what the Irish like to do more than anything else.

COIN OF THE REALM

When I was a young boy my father would take us to Lake Wallenpaupack in the Pocono Mountains of Pennsylvania. Each year we would go there for the last two weeks of August. This was just before autumn and returning to school. We would stay in a cottage on a hillside facing the lake. During the day we would swim, go horseback riding, water-ski and fish off the pier. It seemed that mostly the same people would come each year.

One summer when I was about ten years old all the parents decided to have a barbecue followed by storytelling around a bonfire. This turned out to be a rather exciting prospect for all. There would be a marshmallow roast before the storytelling began. We ate hot dogs, hamburgers and as much ice cream as we wanted. Permission to feast on junk food came rarely in our family, so this was a big deal for us.

One of the other fathers was a professional storyteller. I did not know what that meant, but it sounded impressive. It had gotten dark and chilly, so we formed a circle around the blazing logs. We chattered away while watching the sparks fly out of the fire and smoke billow up toward the star-filled sky. Soon parents started making the shushing sound and then a man was standing next to the fire. He had a beard, which was very strange in those days. My father had warned us to be careful because he might be a communist sympathiser. That was about as bad as you get back then. But my good-humoured mother had told us he was probably just a bohemian, which must have been much less bad.

All I remember is that while he was being introduced as Charlie, the storyteller, I could see the fire reflecting off his beard and in his eyes. Charlie started to tell us about St George and the dragon. We were not at all worried about St George. He was a knight and therefore a good guy, who apparently went about rescuing people from dragons.

It was the dragon that struck terror in our young hearts. The dragon liked to eat people, especially little kids. At the very second he said that, we heard a loud pop, and a glowing red spark jumped out of the fire. Some of the smaller kids began to cry and the hair was standing up on the back of my neck.

Charlie described the dragon's cave. It was full of the bones of children, grown-ups and animals he had eaten. As to some of his more recent victims, there were little bits of meat sticking to the bones because the dragon's mother had never taught him table manners.

Charlie must have noticed that we were frightened out of our wits, because he told us that dragons are scared of bonfires and if we moved closer to the fire we'd be safe. Each kid scrambled closer to the fire. Soon we couldn't tell whether we were sweating because we were scared or because we were about to roast to death. The fire was so hot that we had to pull back from it. But each time we did so, we cast a wary eye toward the ambient blackness.

One of the other fathers suddenly made a loud growling noise and the little kids started to cry again.

Charlie got to the point in the story where St George was trying to rescue the beautiful princess whom the dragon had captured and taken back to his lair.

St George got off his big white horse and was approaching the cave, holding a long spear he had used to kill other dragons. But St George couldn't see the dragon as he entered the cave, because it was very dark inside. He could only smell rotten meat as he tripped over piles of bones.

Then all of a sudden the moon came out from behind the clouds, throwing some light into the cave. There, just three feet in front of St George, stood the dragon with his mouth wide open. The moonlight reflected against all the sharp teeth. The dragon started to spring at St George. But even though his heart was pounding so loudly he could hear it, he stepped out of the way of the oncoming dragon. St George thrust his spear straight into the dragon's heart and killed him instantly.

Charlie looked like a powerful man who knew a lot of secrets about things as he stood there with the fire lighting up his face. He told us that St George found the princess tied up and cut her loose. St George put her up on his white horse with him and galloped away to return the princess to her castle.

All the kids cheered and clapped their hands. At last, the dragon was dead and everyone was safe.

Now why did I tell this story about Charlie, the American storyteller, in the middle of a book about Ireland? Because if I condensed that saga into an emotionless phrase like 'the Irish oral tradition' you would fall asleep. I wanted to make a point. Everyone was mesmerised by Charlie. His words penetrated to the core of our soul.

St Patrick came to Ireland approximately fifteen hundred years ago. This was about the time that monks began to teach the Roman alphabet as prior to this there was no alphabet in Ireland. Irish was a spoken language only. The Irish poets were storytellers and they kept alive the rich treasury of myths.

These poets were worshipped by the people. When they told stories, the people hearing them were enchanted and astounded. The poet heroes taught the Irish that speaking was an art form and that any Irishman worth his salt could speak artfully. This maxim holds true to this day.

The ancient Irish poets created verses that were spoken and chanted. They remembered each word, the metre, the sequence, the tone, the inflection, the cadence. They were empowered with oral magic.

The language they spoke when St Patrick arrived in the fifth century was Irish. Patrick wrote Latin, but he spoke and understood Irish. Even at its historical point of greatest geographic usage, Latin was almost a dead language for Patrick. Yet it was the language he used to tell his life story. This was partly because no one had ever written in Irish. Inventive monks of the sixth century began to impress upon the spoken Irish language the Latin sound symbols. When written down word by word, the Roman alphabet could carry the sound, form and meaning of the Irish language. The language when it was first reduced to writing is known as Old Irish.

Due to the Viking raids, which included the burning and looting of monasteries, written examples of Irish (as well as of Latin) were destroyed. But the poets remembered the stories and passed them onto others who remembered. And the chain of the oral tradition continued despite the destruction of nearly all the early manuscripts.

The poets composed poetry and other forms of verse. Histories, biographies, laws, legends, and genealogies were written in verse. The care and perpetuation of the entire record of the Irish culture was in the hands of the poets. Using verse form to record and transmit this cultural record served as a mnemonic device to assist memory. Irish was an oral language. Its poets were of the druid class. They were intellectual and spiritual leaders of early Irish society. So when the poets said something everyone listened, especially the kings.

The creation and writing of early Irish poetry from the sixth to the twelfth centuries was largely the responsibility of monks, many of whom had been poets prior to entering the monastery. And poets they remained. The language during this six hundred year period was known as Old and Middle Irish. Many of the poems of that period either conveyed a message related to the monk's faith or related to scenes in nature. The measure of a man's worth then was in cows. So respect for nature was no accident. Both types of poems reflect an intense spiritual sensitivity on the part of their monk authors.

The second period of Irish poetry is from the twelfth to the sixteenth centuries and the form of the language used then is known as Classical Modern Irish. The poets at this time came from the lay and hereditary professional class, sometimes called Bardic. They were highly respected within the society and the good ones were well paid. Most of the society was illiterate, so the poets recited the poems. Communication remained predominantly oral.

By the sixteenth century the power and importance of the Irish oral tradition had endured for about two thousand years.

The year 1601 was a watershed in the history of Irish poetry. The Elizabethan conquest occurred that year with the defeat of the Irish forces at the battle of Kinsale. Prior to that time, during the Bardic period, the great Irish noble families supported these poets, as had the kings in previous centuries. Six years after the defeat of the Irish forces at Kinsale the Flight of the Earls took place. The heads of a good number of the Irish noble families fled the country, hoping to form an alliance with Spain in order to regain control of Ireland. The English queen, Elizabeth's, reaction was to declare their flight treasonous and she confiscated their lands.

Other noble families were soon disenfranchised and the system of patronage for poets collapsed because the nobles no longer had the means to support the bards.

Ireland's gene pool had been involved in breeding poets for over two millennia. Just because the political and economic means of support for poetry and poets had collapsed didn't mean poets were no longer born. But instead of sitting well-cared-for at the top of the social and economic heap, they often had to work as common labourers to support their art. What they wrote over the next three centuries was called Poems of the Dispossessed because as a clan the poets had been dispossessed just as their patrons had been dispossessed of their lands and titles.

Aogán Ó Rathaille (1675–1729), one of the dispossessed poets in Kerry, had come from a prosperous family. But times had changed, and as a poet there were no generous and patronising lords left to support him. In Ó Rathaille's poem, translated from his original in Irish, 'The Drenching Night Drags On', he describes the spiritual dejection and poverty-stricken misery he felt as a dispossessed poet.

Ó Rathaille and the other dispossessed poets wrote mainly in Irish, the language the Elizabethan government was seeking to outlaw and obliterate. The theme of many of these poems was suffering rather than glory as so many of their ancestors had written about in centuries past. Their poems helped soothe the souls of a nation that was having its Irishness hacked away by the Elizabethan conquerors and their English ruling successors. The poems were read by the poets, often as lamentations. Some of their poems were sung and became part of the rich Irish musical tradition.

One might ask what is the point of placing so much emphasis on the fact of an enduring Irish oral tradition? With the possible exception of traders making notations in Latin, until St Patrick and his successors brought Latin writing to Ireland there was no writing of any kind except Ogham, an alphabetical 'Morse code', chiselled mainly onto grave or boundary markers. Essentially no one but the monks could read or write, and not every monk was literate. Vellum annals were kept in certain monasteries. These were usually very brief accounts of important births, deaths, or battles.

There were no newspapers or printed books, the spoken language was Irish, the written language was normally Latin and the printing press was not invented until the middle of the fifteenth century. The only way one could retain information was to listen very carefully and remember nearly everything. The kings had their poets chronicle and recall important events, but their success as rulers depended upon listening and remembering well. Also, one learned to speak with a tactical awareness of whether one would be better served by clarity or ambiguity. Ancient Irish myths and legends contain splendid examples of both.

What happens to a society whose survival for generations is dependent upon verbal communication? Speaking, listening, and remembering became an art form practised successfully by nearly every member of society. The invention of the printing press, education of the masses and the gradual expansion of literacy did not automatically undo Irish verbal communication skills.

During the eighteenth and nineteenth centuries the oral tradition in Ireland was passed on in part by the *seanchaí*. One can imagine that many a *seanchaí* emerged from the gene pool of ancient Irish poets. Until well into the twentieth century, a significant portion of rural Ireland was too poor to purchase many books. So instead, the country people sat around the fireside and listened to the *seanchaí* tell stories. There are thousands of Irish people alive today who can tell you that as children they would ascend the stairs with terror having heard a *seanchaí* tell a ghost story.

Even though radio and television gradually evicted the fire-side storyteller, there are still quite a few Irish storytellers around who are listened to either in parish festivals, in pubs, or in hotels catering to tourists. Radio and television did not destroy the oral tradition in Ireland; it just transferred it from the fireplace to the studios.

When you tune into your car radio while driving along Irish roads you are bound to hear a lot of talking. Not only from the announcers and studio guests who love to chatter away, but from people calling in to voice their opinions on every subject under the sun. Several years ago an elderly priest in County Leitrim preached a sermon on how Ireland's gold medal winning, world-class, distance runner was 'a common slut' because her child was born out of wedlock. The story was front-page news for a week and the feature of nearly every talk show on Irish radio and television. A few of the white-haired, daily Mass-goers supported the loose-tongued priest. But most disagreed strongly.

When you hear talk like that on the radio or in a pub, you realise the power of the spoken word in Ireland remains paramount. The Irish are quick to speak out against any wrong they feel is being perpetrated.

As improbable as it may seem, a clue to understanding the way the Irish talk can be found in studying the Irish skies and examining the structure of traditional Irish music.

Irish skies are like traditional Irish music, full of contrasting rhythms, shifting melodies, undulating harmonies, all loosely braided together into infinitely repetitive cycles.

Meteorologists call the lowest level of cloud cover 'the ceiling' as if the sky formed the top of a giant room. When the ceiling is low and the dark grey stratus clouds are pressing down, your mood can easily become despondent. But when the ceiling lifts and is replaced by chunks of lamb's wool, your spirit can soar.

Irish conversations are like Irish skies. The people talking to one another jump from one cloud layer to the next almost without noticing that a spatial shift has taken place. Just as they move effortlessly up, down and around, as do various layers of clouds, Irish conversations additionally make similar shifts in time.

One person will be talking about how her daughter, Bridget, ran into a sheep farmer named Dinny while shopping for groceries at the local supermarket. This will remind another that Dinny's great-great-great grandfather was murdered by his own wife's conniving. He was fifty-four and she was only twenty when they were married in 1829. Within a year the wife took on a lover her own age and persuaded him to bludgeon her husband to death on the boreen while making his way home from Mass one Sunday. Since the husband normally walked his eight-year-old daughter, from a previous marriage, to Mass, the wife hid the girl's only pair of shoes in the milk churn so she'd have to stay at home.

Time will suddenly shift from one hundred and seventy years ago to last Sunday's All Ireland Hurling Championship Match. Someone will mention that Malachy, Dinny the sheep farmer's cousin, was a hurler playing for the Kilkenny team and that Dinny had bet two thousand pounds on Kilkenny to win, only to lose the whole wad as Cork had won. Then someone will say, 'I wondered why Dinny was walking around town with that fierce disappointed look on his face.'

Next someone will ask, 'Did they ever convict the wife?'

'She and her lover were hanged in Tralee in 1830. The daughter was raised by her Aunt Gráinne from Killarney, and the daughter ended up marrying Niall O'Leary who was himself Deirdre, the hairdresser's, grandfather. God rest his soul. He is dead now sixty-two years.'

'Was it Deirdre's dog that was run over by a car last September and wasn't the dog just after dying when Dinny gave Deirdre one of his sheepdog pups?'

'It was. My daughter Bridget put him up to it.'

The Irish conversation, like the Irish sky, not only contains various cloud strewn layers of shifting space, but such talk bends time, jumping generations in a single breath.

The late Dorothy Walker, one of Ireland's leading authorities on modern art, explained the structure of Irish conversation in her book on Louis le Brocquy, who, despite his grandfather's Belgian surname, is known throughout Europe as a famous Irish painter. Her introduction to the book opened with, '"Begin at the beginning," said the King of Hearts to the White Rabbit, "and go on till you come to the end; then stop." That simple instruction is anathema to the Irish mind, which traditionally prefers to begin in the middle and continue in a circle so that it never reaches the end.'

Does beginning in the middle and continuing in a circle so the story never reaches the end hold the only key to understanding why listening to Irish conversations can be so mesmerising? The contents and structure of the conversation contain a few clues.

One obvious element pertains to Irish names. A multitude of Irish first names are derived from saints and from Irish mythology. From the pagan myths of Ireland we inherited names like Conor, Diarmuid and Fergus, along with Aoife, Deirdre and Gráinne. It could be argued that the power in these names, whether of saintly or pagan origin, links the holder to an ancient past which has remained somehow alive through the repetition of stories.

Having considered some names for people we can now turn to names for places. The woman and her lover were hanged in Tralee, the county seat of Kerry. The prefix Tra, or *Tráigh* in Irish, means beach and lee, or *Lí* in Irish, refers to the River Lee. Thus, Tralee is the beach of the River Lee. Most place names are made up of Irish prefixes or suffixes which have definite meanings attached to them. For example, Ardfert is a very ancient Irish village. *Ard* in Irish means high place. *Fert* means grave. Other Irish place names link a place to the name of a person. Dun Laoghaire does just that. *Dún* is one name for fort. Laoghaire is the Irish version of the more anglicised Leary.

By obtaining a glossary of place name roots one can learn a lot about the origins of nearly any town in Ireland without having first to learn Irish. There is a certain intrigue about many Irish place names. Centuries ago people decided to give the place where they lived a simple name. They found the right words that became the name. The contemporary inhabitants of these places cannot disconnect themselves from these historical namings, to the contrary, they feel deeply linked to place.

To return to the conversation about Bridget in the supermarket: one part of all that talk was about relationships. In addition to ancient names and places, we encountered daughter, grand-daughter, aunt, mother, cousin, father, grandfather, great-grandfather, great-great-grandfather, great-great-great-grandfather.

The surname prefix 'Mac' means son. The prefix 'Ó' means descendant. Building a blood relationship into so many surnames must have meant that relationships were once quite important in Ireland. Indeed, they still are. A large part of a person's identity in Ireland is linked to such relationships. The fact that many of the Mac and Ó prefixes derived from Irish chieftains or kings who were from a particular locality meant necessarily that all the descendants kept the same name. When most of the descendants stayed in the same area, quite a few of them understandably ended up with a common surname.

For example, in South Kerry the surnames O'Sullivan, O'Shea, McCarthy, among others, are quite common. In the conversation above, Dinny and Deirdre could have had such common last names. Dinny, a diminutive of Denis, was referred to as the sheepfarmer, while Deirdre was linked to her occupation as hairdresser. Relationship to place, persons and job is often crucial to a rural individual's identity.

I once knew a farmer named Murty, who lived in a townland with fourteen other Murtys, all with the same surname. To avoid confusion he ended up with the names Murty Mike Pat Mary Stephen preceding his surname.

Listening to an Irish conversation can be exciting because it is usually full of action, expression and emphasis, if not an imaginative touch of hyperbole.

In Ireland it is frowned upon if you complain or criticise. This is known as 'giving out'. The Irish don't like people who are always giving out. They prefer to handle such matters cheerfully and tactfully. That is why it is best to begin the conversation with a positive spin on the weather, ramble on about inanities for a while, then as a by the way, gently raise the issue in an almost apologetic manner.

Another reason why English spoken the Irish way can be fascinating, is that some words may sound different compared to what you might otherwise expect. An Irish conversation often contains some English words that have become anachronistic or archaic in other English-speaking countries. Quite a few of these words were introduced to Ireland by English land-holders in the sixteenth century. Some of these words, outside of Ireland, are found only in dictionaries and are no longer in common usage. Yet the Irish have kept them alive and use them with some frequency.

My treasure is 'blackguard', pronounced blaggard, which can be used as a noun or a verb. A blackguard in Elizabethan English referred to the black devils who guard the gates of Hell. Thus, when it comes to achieving the zenith of badness, one can do no worse than be recognised as a blackguard. The evil-doing is known in its verb or gerund form as 'blackguarding'.

Hearing this word spoken, and others like it as part of a modern-day Irish conversation, might cause you to suspect that the narrator has just stepped out of either a Shakespearean play or the Bible. Although one hears the word 'you' used sometimes in Ireland as the second person singular, one rarely hears it used as the second person plural. Instead, this will be 'ye' or 'yous'.

More favourites are cross and mean. Cross is used in Ireland to mean angry. Mean is the principal word employed to denote stingy.

Other words which sound archaic, but are still very exciting to hear when expressed in an Irish accent, include 'asunder', 'bar', 'save' and 'frock'. To describe an old piece of equipment as falling apart, an Irishman might say 'falling asunder'. Instead of saying, 'No one arrived on time, except Mary', in Ireland 'save' or 'bar' is often used in place of 'except'. 'Frock' refers to a woman's dress. One of my favourite un-archaic Irish words is 'banjaxed', which means fouled up.

Himself, herself, yourself are words of emphasis. Is that yourself? This means – Is that really you? Is himself at home? This is a way to ask if the man of the house is on the premises.

Three emphatic favourites of mine are 'stone dead', 'dead on' and 'stone mad'. The first means more than as lifeless as a stone. While 'dead on' means highly accurate, the reference to dead in this context seems a bit elusive. 'Stone mad' means certifiably insane.

Some English words, which have a very definite meaning, will be used in Ireland to mean something entirely different. This could be because the usage is elsewhere considered archaic. Or it could come from an Irish word still in common use, which at the time it was translated into English meant something slightly different than the word's present meaning. Which of these two categories, if either, applies to the word 'bold' I am unable to discern. The Irish use the word *dána* when speaking Irish to mean the same thing as they do when they use the word 'bold' in English. It means naughty, mischievous, or misbehaved and usually is applied in the context of scolding a child or making reference to an adult acting like a naughty child.

There are a number of words from the Irish language that have found their way into English as spoken in Ireland. The linguistic terms for such words are Hiberno-English or Anglo-Irish. Both mean the same thing, but the former, perhaps as a matter of national pride, puts Irish before English, Hiberno being a synonym for Irish. Linguists refer to Irish words used when speaking English as loan words. Many seem to have gone beyond the loan stage and matured into permanent acquisitions.

In the case of the husband, 'poor craythur', bludgeoned to death in 1830 on a 'boreen' as he made his way home from Mass, we have discovered two such loan words. Craythur comes from the Irish word *créatúr*, which itself could have been borrowed several centuries earlier by the Irish from the English word 'creature'. Boreen means a small, single-lane, country road. The letters 'een' are normally found as a suffix in Irish words to mean either small or to suggest a diminutive meaning. Other common examples are shebeen, a small rural pub; poteen, illegal alcohol made from potatoes; kippeen, a small stick or twig used for kindling a fire; and capeen, a small cap or a small cloud stuck on the top of the mountain like a cap.

Among the several Irish words that have made their way into English spoken nearly everywhere a few stand out in my mind: curragh and keen. These respectively mean a rowboat made out of tarred canvas stretched over a wooden frame; and a verb meaning to wail like a banshee. Shamrock and whiskey are on loan from the Irish and need no further explanation. *Sláinte* (pronounced shlahntuh) is the toast word, meaning good health. The origin of the word 'hooley' is unknown, but it means the type of party at which people do some heavy drinking and have lots of fun. In other words, a normal Irish party.

The pronunciation of words in Ireland makes up part of the music that is also related to accent, inflection and cadence. We start with the vowels and soon recognise that these often sound different from the way we are accustomed to hearing them. In Ireland we may hear tea as tay, weak as wake, calm as caahm, cook as kuke, forty as farty, queer as kwaire, easy as aisy, and the 'u' in 'but' is pronounced the same as we may say 'put'.

As to consonants, there is no 'th' sound in Irish, so in English it also often comes out as if the word has no 'h' in it. Third comes out as turd and thumb as tum. Likewise, the Irish 's' is often pronounced as 'sh', so bless is said as if it were 'blesh'. Both vocabulary and pronunciation vary regionally and by social class throughout Ireland. Accordingly, some of the examples I've heard in Kerry might not be heard elsewhere. On the other hand, 'film' in Ireland is nearly universally pronounced as 'fill-um'.

Also absent from the Irish language are the words yes and no. Yes is expressed by repeating the verb in the question: such as, 'Was it Deirdre's dog that was run over by a car last September?' Answer: 'It was'. But in some cases the affirmative answer is not expected initially to be given. This bit of Irish etiquette requires some context in order to grasp. 'Would you have a cup of tea?' A grammatically correct, but impolite answer could be: 'I would, thank you'. Usually an Irish person would never provide an affirmative answer that quickly or directly. He or she would at first decline. The exchange would normally proceed along these lines:

'Would you have a cup of tea?'

'I'm just after a big feed.'

'Do have another cup then, won't you?'

'I couldn't.'

'Will you have a drop, then?'

'I wouldn't. I really shouldn't.'

'You will, sure? Ah g'wan, do.'

'Just a drop, if it would be no bother.'

'Ah g'wan, do', of course, means, Oh go on, do. 'G'wan' is also used in a dialogue during which the other person may not agree with you, but wants to be polite enough to ask that you continue. It also means 'go away, I don't believe a word you're saying'.

The 'drop', of course, refers to liquid spirits. If you have an Irish guest for dinner and ask the person, 'Would you like some more meat?' the most affirmative answer you could ever expect would be, 'I don't mind'. So to avoid the prolonged hassle associated with the ping-pong of Irish etiquette, it's best to reach for the guest's dinner plate with another slab of beef and hesitate only if you hear, 'I couldn't possibly.' But be careful, because under certain circumstances that too could mean yes.

Another ear catcher is 'I'm just *after* a big feed' or 'I'm just *after* standing up from the table.' The Irish language does not contain a past participle. There is no way in Irish literally to say, 'I have just drunk a cup of tea'. So it comes out, 'I am just after drinking my tea'. Here the verb 'to be' is used in conjunction with the preposition 'after'. That is why to non-Irish ears it sounds slightly strange to hear a person say, 'I'm sorry I can't join you for dinner this evening; my uncle is just after dying'. Irish linguists have written reams on these fine points and you can even buy dictionaries on the subject if you are so inclined. You can walk into any good bookstore and purchase either *A Dictionary of Hiberno-English*, or *A Dictionary of Anglo-Irish*.

One short example may suffice to show that the phrases, idiomatic expressions and slang used by the Irish are also full of invention and brilliant creativity. One day when I was driving down a winding boreen with a mason who was helping me re-store my house, we found ourselves behind a car that was being driven very, very slowly by a woman who seemed not to feel at all confident about her road skills. So we were impatiently following from only a few feet behind. The old man sitting in the passenger seat next to the driver ahead had a set of ears on him that would put an elephant to shame. I remarked on this. The mason responded, 'When they were giving out ears, your man wasn't standing behind the door, I'll tell ye'.

Despite being conquered, the Irish resisted the Vikings, Normans and English. Over time they reasonably well acculturated the first two invader peoples including teaching them to speak Irish. The Irish resisted learning English, but managed to teach many English settlers Irish. But over time the English ground the Irish down, forcing them to learn English. In 1800, out of a population of five million in Ireland, the Irish language alone was spoken by two million; one and a half million spoke only English, while another million and a half were bilingual. The English at that time regarded Irish as pagan speech.

There is now hardly a person in Ireland who speaks only

Irish and there are very few enclaves in the country in which Irish is the preferred language. The history of this battle between the Irish resisting the English language and the British seeking to ram it down Irish throats is fascinating and complicated. The battle involved: much legislation which sought to coerce the Irish into learning English, political and economic bribery, the famine, the Catholic Church which ultimately was won over to English, assorted punishments, cajolery and harsh educational policies. Although the world may think that England finally won the language battle with Ireland, it didn't. It is not the king's English which is spoken in Ireland, but Hiberno-English.

This wonderful speech, only parts of which appear in writing, falls somewhere between a dialect and a language. More aptly perhaps, it is a verbal way of life – the coin of the realm.

It is the principal means by which the Irish connect themselves to one another. The Irish don't talk at you. They converse with you. Conversing is connecting, but not intruding. This is a subtle, but crucial, distinction. When one conversationally connects to another, souls become engaged. This engagement is of a gentle, ungrasping kind. The listener is not smothered or browbeaten.

Not only are the words usually well and diplomatically chosen, but the tone is enchanting. It tends to induce a pleasant response. You can usually infer from the tone that the mood of the conversants is quite genial and friendly. Just hearing the tone alone is likely to have a soul-soothing effect upon you.

Sensitivity to tone is even greater when speaking in public or during radio or television interviews. The winners of the Gaelic Athletic Association's hurling or football matches are expected to be humble and gracious in triumph. Thus, when the coach or star player of the winning team is interviewed after a big victory he is expected to be self effacing and to compliment the losing team for waging such a determined battle. Bragging is regarded as poor sportsmanship. During the 2000 Sydney Olympics an Irish TV sports announcer was repulsed by the fist-shaking, hostile exuberance of an American swimmer who had just broken a world record. The announcer sardonically commented, 'It's always nice to see such a gracious winner.' Graciousness is the hallmark of most Irish conversations, public and private.

The Irish love talking. But it is not just a string of ill-conceived, disorganised, soulless words that come out of an Irishman's mouth – that the English for years have referred to as blarney. The late John B. Keane, one of the greatest Irish writers and conversationalists of the twentieth century, observed that 'long, dull sentences, especially religious and political, are anathema to the true Kerryman. The wellmade, craftily calefacted comment, the stinging riposte and the verbal arrows of cold truth always penetrate the armor of cant and hypocrisy ...' Speaking is a semi-sacred craft in Ireland. Care is taken about what is said. The objective is to get the point across by intimation. It is better to disclose too little than too much.

Many Irish are such good listeners that they can tell you, months after the conversation, nearly word for word what you told them. Also, when an Irish person is speaking with you, he or she is not only carefully crafting each word, but at the same time is probably tuning into you with such sensitivity and intensity as to be able to gauge whether you're listening, whether you care, whether you believe what is being said. This is doing two jobs at once: articulating, while simultaneously detecting the quality of your receptivity.

I can't think of a better example of this than when my friend Denis senses I'm not listening carefully to what he is saying, he'll instinctively tap me a couple of times on the forearm with the back of his hand. Every time he has done that I've realised that my mind, in fact, had indeed begun to wander.

One additional important thing an Irish person frequently does while conversing is to anticipate your likely reaction in order to plan various options for how he or she will respond. Sometimes this process starts before you can even open your mouth. There is a balancing act going on here that entails some give and some take. But also an instinct for gently preserving face. For your everyday Irishman, participating in a conversation is as intricate and intimate as holding a newborn baby. Such a well-honed sensitivity suggests a personality in touch with its soul.

RELIGION ON THE ROCKS

I was waiting for a fifty-four-year-old scholar monk from Philadelphia at Dublin airport. The monk was in Ireland to research
an icon of Mary of Egypt and to take a short break before returning to America. He teaches a year-long graduate-level seminar
on the classics of Christian Spirituality. The texts he uses range
from the writings of Clement of Rome in the first century, to
those of St Therese of Liseux in the nineteenth. His course is a
two thousand year voyage through the hearts and altered mind
states of those often half-mad spiritual explorers bent upon
steeping themselves in divine mysteries. In America, when one
studies arcane texts of ancient mystical writings, one gets the
feeling that they were written 'over there somewhere' a very
long time ago. But in Ireland one can easily find written and
archaeological evidence of a very visible continuum of the life of
the Church from its origins to the present.

That is one of the reasons why we chose to tour the Rock of
Cashel on the way from Dublin. Cashel is located in County
Tipperary, just east of County Limerick. These two counties, plus
Clare, Kerry, Cork and Waterford, constitute the province of
Munster. Sometime before Christianity was introduced to Ire-

land, the kings of Munster ruled from the mighty Rock of Cashel, which is a four-acre island of stone rising over a hundred feet above the adjacent pasture land. The rock provided the foundation for a perfect fortress used by the frequently warring kings of Munster. It afforded them a clear panorama extending for miles in all directions. Yet for some reason this imposing military headquarters was given in 1101 to the Church which chose to build upon it a round tower, chapel and eventually a cathedral. In 1141 Cashel became one of Ireland's four archbishoprics.

These once stunning ecclesiastical monuments are now sky-high ruins in various states of restoration. One can obtain an auditory glimpse of the history of the rock by listening to the tour guide as she escorts groups of visitors around the site. In the now roofless cathedral, she points out a tiny slanted opening in the wall above the nave where, from their confined and isolated corridor, lepers were given a restricted view of the high altar without infecting, or being observed by, the more healthy parishioners below. The guide also spoke with some amusement about one of Cashel's Catholic bishops who concomitantly served as a Protestant bishop in another county!

If the Cashel visitor is intent upon finding evidence of a more spiritual character upon the great rock, there are indeed a few jewels left to be seen. The Vicar's Choral, built in 1420 to house monks who served as cantors in the cathedral, contains exquisitely carved shield-bearing angels mounted on the walls of the great hall where the choir rehearsed. Carved stone heads decorate the Romanesque archway above the inner entrance to the still-standing Cormac's Chapel, consecrated in 1134. These heads suggest not only icon-like images of ascetic monks' faces, but also the ghoulish Celtic cult of mounting the heads of slain enemies.

Perhaps the mystery of these twelfth-century heads carved into an arch at Cormac's Chapel is what inspired a local Cashel potter, Sarah Ryan, to reproduce them in stoneware for hanging on the walls of one's home. Staring fixedly at her replicas can almost launch one into a transcendental mind state.

From Cashel we drove to our destination, a nearby abbey, where the monks still chant in five daily offices much the way monks did on the rock nearly a thousand years earlier. Twenty-five times a day, for every day of their monkish lives, they drone,

'Glory be to the Father and the Son and the Holy Spirit; as it was in the beginning, is now and forever shall be'. The scholar monk said, 'This is simply a way of Christianising the Hebrew psalms chanted as canticles'.

We were greeted by a kindly brother, whose string of jokes and anecdotal witticisms is longer than rosary beads. I was shown to the suite reserved for visiting bishops, with a private bath and elaborately carved, somewhat grandiose, antique desk. I asked the brother if I should offer to move to the more spartan room assigned to the visiting monk. 'No need,' he said, 'He's a monk and quite accustomed to such quarters.'

The monks at the abbey remain silent during the evening meal in order to listen to a section of their founder's rule being read to them. After that, usually one of the monks will read from a book selected or approved by the abbot. At our Saturday evening supper the rule on greed was read. Its author eschewed greediness and he ordered the sanction of severe punishment for any monk who persisted in practising that forbidden trait.

During July the book being read at the evening meal had been Mary Kenny's *Goodbye to Catholic Ireland*, which catalogues, among other embarrassments, the binge of Irish clerical malefactions. Recent scandals include bishops and priests fathering children and then secretly using Church funds to support them, paedophile priests buggering innocent young schoolboys, homosexual priests gathering at their Dublin sauna club. Lesser offences, not detailed in the book, pertain, in part, to the many Irish parish priests who sit alone in their presbyteries, drinking themselves into oblivion.

Irish reaction to the moral corruption within the Church has been mixed. Among the faithful, a surprising number deny that much damage has been done, despite the proliferation of additional horror stories that continue to be well publicised. Others feel betrayed and have lost respect for the Church, but they continue to attend Mass and sometimes have good words to say about their own local parish priest.

Many have left the Church or remain only nominal parishioners. This is not only because of the clerical scandals, but also because of their disagreement with the Church's teaching on birth control, divorce, abortion and other matters. Quite a few feel that the Church has refused to come to grips with either moral decay within or the damage such clerical abuses have inflicted on the society as a whole. There has never been a public admission of culpability by the head of the Church in Ireland.

It is easy to imagine how such horrendous abuses of trust coupled with heinous physical assaults have engendered interminable suffering among those it directly affected, let alone those affected less directly.

I have come to know others in Ireland who were sexually abused by paedophile priests. One of them had lived in an orphanage run by the Church. He told me that he was brutally violated countless times by the school priest. He was threatened by the priest to reveal nothing of the repeated incidents. The victim said, 'There was no one to turn to for help. I was absolutely alone and helpless.' He has kept in touch with some of his schoolmates who were also abused, and they get together sometimes to talk about their lives and their hurts.

Several who married, he said, reported feeling like 'sick animals'. They doubted their ability to be adequate and loving husbands and fathers, because they feel so disconnected from what they had hoped would be a 'normal' life. Each schoolmate, whether now married or single, including himself, suffers from recurrent nightmares.

These atrocities instituted by paedophile priests have adversely affected not only innocent children, but their parents, brothers and sisters, and eventually their wives, lovers, children and friends. It has also affected the lives of many priests and those in religious orders – the innocent as well as the guilty. For how many generations the effects of those atrocities will endure, no one can predict.

Before the Church can regain its position as the spiritual leader of Ireland, a cleansing must take place. Then it is possible that forgiveness, reconciliation and healing may follow. It is hoped that the Commission to Inquire into Child Abuse may play an effective part in instituting this much-needed cleansing.

During dinner at the monastery a Mozart *Divertimento* was playing. How satisfying it was, sitting at a long refectory table surrounded by black-robed monks concentrating mainly on their supper while rhythmically nodding their heads to the Mozartian sweetness.

After supper the abbot asked that I join him and the American monk for a walk through the monastery's grounds. As we ambled down a fern bordered lane running through a wood, we could hear the evening chatter of birds. We became raptly aware of the natural beauty, and out of this our conversation turned to spirituality. I asked the abbot how, considering the repetitious daily routine of the monastic lifestyle, he managed to inculcate a sense of mystical awe among his monks. The abbot candidly said, 'Survival of the monastic way of life depends upon fulfilling the need for enlivened authenticity in contrast to repetitious drivel. It becomes harder and harder to organise a spiritual retreat for our monks despite the reputation of some highly regarded retreat leaders. It is so difficult to find a person who can truly enliven.'

The evening vigil gospel dealt with Jesus sending the Twelve out to minister in pairs, giving them authority over unclean spirits. Unclean spirits seems to have lost its once undoubtedly cosmologically pithy meaning. Unclean spirits have been replaced by neurological or psychiatric 'disorders'.

My mind began to wander. I recalled how at 5 a.m. one morning, I climbed Croagh Patrick, the 2,500-foot high rocky, damp, fog-shrouded, holy mountain in County Mayo – along with forty thousand others, the most masochistic of whom did it barefooted. I hiked up the mountain with five Tipperary farmers in their sixties who farted, grunted and cursed all the way up the tortuous path. When we arrived at the summit in time for 8 a.m. Mass, one of my companions exclaimed, 'Surely after all this suffering I can afford to be drunk every night and shag myself flat with every whore in town for the next three months and still be ahead in the ledger book above.'

I began to wonder how the young novices were going to avoid the five-year bolt (about five years after their initial vows, many young monks decide not to take their final vows). Until the late twentieth century the doctrine of concupiscence reigned unchallenged in Ireland. This doctrine holds that while the mind and spirit are of God, the flesh is inherently weak, evil and full of lust. The famous St Kevin, who founded a monastery at Glendalough, County Wicklow, was recognised as a saint in part for drowning a lusty woman who sought to seduce him.

Gerald of Wales, a twelfth century monk, wrote: 'St Kevin was distinguished for his life and sanctity at Glendalough.'[12] During Lent one year, Kevin was praying intently. 'He put his hand, in raising it to heaven, out through the window, when, behold, a blackbird happened to settle on it, and using it as a nest, laid its eggs there. The saint was moved with such pity and was so patient with it that he neither closed nor withdrew his hand, but held it out in a suitable position without tiring until the young were completely hatched out.' Clearly, Kevin showed more patience with the blackbird and her fledglings than he did with the lusty woman.

In Ireland and other countries young monks in training are choosing to leave the cloistered life. Without losing their faith entirely, they seem willing to conclude that God would love them just as much when they are non-celibates, no longer having to prove their faith by denying themselves so many earthly pleasures.

The next morning at seven, I again walked into the choir stalls to find the same monks I had seen the previous evening. Only at this early hour they were mostly yawning and wiping their eyes.

Sitting next to me in the choir stall, among all those grey-haired monks, was a solitary seventeen-year-old lad named Paul. He said he intended to enter a religious order because his heart had led him there and the peace of the monastic life comforts him, gives him great pleasure and calms his soul. I didn't anticipate at the time that upon future visits to the abbey I would meet some new young novices, grounded, level-headed, yet determined to know God. Perhaps the monastic pendulum has nearly reached the end of its self-destructive swing and a new form of spiritual growth is about to emerge for a new generation of spirit-seeking monks.

I later asked the abbot what chance an average novice has in sticking it out to final vows. He said one in ten aspirants become novices; four out of ten novices make it to final vows.

'What does the monastic life have to offer to young people?' The monk from Philadelphia said, 'The ones who want balance stay; the ones who want more excitement, new stimulation and variety, leave. Monastic life is not a life of tremendous variety and diversity. One day's activities will be like any other's. The focus is on the interior rather than the exterior journey. We find the Spirit in the liturgy, in Scripture, in contemplation, in doing the same work every day almost without variety. The balance is in integrating physical work with mystical contemplation.'

Later that morning the American monk and I left our monastic hosts at the abbey to drive south toward Skellig Michael, eight miles out into the North Atlantic, off the Kerry coast.

It was as if the monk, his two friends whom we joined in Kerry, and I were keeping our own vigil. At Caherdaniel we climbed aboard the boat to take us to the Great Skellig, or Skellig Rock, but the voyage was cancelled before we could leave the pier. The heavens were dumping down rain. The wind was gusting spasmodically. The mighty Atlantic was slamming its huge waves against the Great Skellig. There was no way to land the boat at Skellig Rock without smashing it to pieces in the process.

The next morning the weather was still too fierce, so the monk and his two friends headed to Tipperary.

A week later, when our next guest arrived, we made it to Skellig Michael – a mammoth rocky outcrop protruding over seven hundred feet toward the sky from the ocean's surface. The only buildings on Skellig are a handful of little mortarless stone cloghans (beehive huts) and an oratory at its peak.

The nearby Little Skellig houses over twenty thousand pairs of gannets, seabirds whose white wings are longer than their legs, thus forcing them to dive off cliffs to become airborne.

Our house guest was the widow of a lifelong friend who had been an Episcopalian priest and who was very unorthodox in his approach to spiritual things. Having graduated from the University of Chicago in Philosophy, he joined the United States Navy and worked in Explosive Ordinance Disposal. He regarded much of Church doctrine as next to meaningless. He believed in an unfathomable Creator, the power of love and the duty to do justice. He preached from his heart without text or notes, often moving people who heard him to see total strangers as their brothers. Had he lived fourteen centuries earlier, his character, imagination and originality could have qualified him to found the monastery on Skellig Rock.

It was his widow, not he, who climbed to the top of Skellig

Michael and saw the gannets, fulmers and kittywakes soar around and above the rocky island's high cliffs, carried along by the ascending air currents reaching up from the sea. His widow saw the orange-billed puffins, nesting in burrows along the six hundred-plus steps leading from sea level to summit. She heard the continuous screeching of these birds and the rhythmic bass note collisions of waves with the island's stony sides.

Our guide at Skellig Michael turned out to be an American who had fallen in love with Ireland, taken an Irish wife, and chosen Ireland as his home. Each summer he spends three weeks at a time living and working on Skellig Michael, followed by a week off to rejoin his family on the mainland. Standing next to the ancient oratory high above the foaming sea below, he said, 'If you were a monk living here fourteen centuries ago and looked up at a soaring gannet, you would have known you were seeing God.'

I looked up from the summit of Skellig Michael to observe a gannet gliding toward me on an air current. As the gannet dropped a wing to make a banking turn, about eight feet above me, his left eye caught mine.

For that timeless instant I felt an inkling that the gannet and I had been privileged to enjoy a silent telepathic conversation about the Eternal Now.

THE OTHER WORLD

A monocosmic experience is notably different from the realms described by some of our more stalwart theologians as 'wholly and totally other'.

The notion of an Eternal Now is not new in Ireland. It shares space with material reality. Within that universe co-exist the mundane and what the Irish call the other world. Coming to grips with the other world presents us with several choices. We can ignore it, deny it, accept it or apologise about it. The branch of theology responsible for defending the Christian faith is called apologetics. Their job is to defend the faith by creating arguments which would lead you to believe in the reality of the Trinity. But Christian apologists have not written about the other world in the Irish sense of the term. Under the circumstances, that leaves me with the responsibility for constructing an apology for the other world.

One summer day about twenty-five years ago I was driving west on the Beara Peninsula in County Cork, wondering if there was anything about the physical environment of Ireland that could have influenced the ancient Irish to believe that the gods were close to them. I found a place to take in a view of the nearby Atlantic Ocean and the surrounding mountainous landscape.

I sat on a nice flat boulder of red sandstone over four hundred million years old located in a meadow facing the sea. I could feel the sun's warmth on the surface of the boulder. I peered out into the Atlantic and saw islands in the distance. All around me in the meadow were projections of red sandstone full of cracks and fissures. This close to the sea no trees could grow because the Atlantic winds often blow too hard. So the ground cover consisted of grass, ferns and scrub. The absence of trees seemed to create a primeval starkness, almost a grandeur of sorts.

I looked up again toward the horizon and saw a white cloud sliding down from the top of a mountain, enveloping its near side in fog. Then I noticed the islands again. The sun was shining directly on them and they sparkled in the sea like emeralds.

I looked back towards the mountains and saw that one ridge seemed to blend into the next in all that distant haze. I noticed only the barest suggestion of islands within the mist that had suddenly surrounded them. There were no clear boundaries between what was visible and invisible.

Ten minutes later the sun had caused the mist to disperse and evaporate. It was now brightly hitting the side of the mountain exposing the glistening natural springs of water that were bubbling out of bare rock.

There is something magic about the landscape, the way it changes from minute to minute. The visible suddenly becomes invisible, then returns again as if under the control of spirit beings. If you relax and let the panoramic phantasmagoria speak to you, your consciousness may click into a realm of fantasy, where charms, magic and mystery all dwell contentedly together. This allows your rational mind to let itself lapse into a semi-stupor so your child's mind can awaken and listen. The child's mind is fuelled with curiosity and a belief that all things are possible.

George Russell (or Æ) was a contemporary and friend of the Irish poet, William Butler Yeats. Starting when Russell was a teenager, he would look at the hills and they would come alive for him because he had the second sight, also called the sixth sense. His book, *The Candle of Vision*, published in 1918, tells how he came to see and understand the other world and he describes what he calls visions or apparitions. Russell had a monocosmic sense of reality. Fairies and other spirit beings were real to him.

Russell walked down lanes scented by honeysuckle sensing that spirit beings were on the move and aware of his presence and ready to unveil to him the nature of the other world. He spoke of the world he lived in as 'a tapestry blown and stirred by winds behind it. If it would but raise for an instant I knew I would be in Paradise. Every form on that tapestry appeared to be the work of gods … I knew the Golden Age was all about me, and it was we who had been blind to it but that it had never passed away from the world.' Russell described a kaleidoscope of lights, faces, beautiful landscapes and a glowing golden-haired figure carrying a harp. He felt that people needed to be more open to other worlds and that 'we can learn more from these voyages to the Heaven-world, more of the geography of the spirit and the many mansions in the being of the Father than we can from the greatest of our sightless philosophers.'

Russell's visions show us a number of things to be aware of regarding the other world. He saw it every day and it was part of his monocosmic way of looking at the world. What he saw and the way he saw it sounds like what has been recorded about the other world in Irish myths and legends. The way Russell saw seems exactly the way the druid seer-poets of ancient Ireland must have seen the other world.

Kathleen Hughes, a respected Celtic scholar, indicates her sense of pre-Christian Celtic cosmology in Ireland by identifying a pervasive 'consciousness of the supernatural'. The druid-class storytellers, who preserved and passed on the great myths, 'move from reality to magic as if they do not recognise any boundary. There are visitors from the *síd* (pronounced shee), where a man may enter a fairy dwelling, or have a fairy lover. The poet [*filid*] was also a "seer", so that vision and prophecy were his proper medium.'[13]

W. B. Yeats sketched the ephemeral cosmology that emerged from the ancient myths of Ireland. He said that people believed that trees and animals were divine, and could change shape and form. They saw the divine in everything and 'they dreamed of so great a mystery in little things that they believed the waving of a hand, or of a sacred bough, enough to trouble far-off hearts, or hood the moon with darkness.'[14]

Where is the 'other world'? Is there more than one such world in Irish mythology? Is it the land under the sea, or an island beyond the horizon? Two other Celtic scholars, Alwyn and Brinley Rees, suggest that 'a mist falls on us in an open plain, and lo, we are witnessing its wonders. We go to sleep in the enchanted land and by morning all has disappeared.'[15]

Among the gods in Irish mythology and among the people in Irish history dwelled the druids, some of whom were known as seers because of their prescient powers. They were the clairvoyant diviners. Druids could also conjure spirits, become infused by spirits, and change into spirit form, among other varieties of shape shifting.

A visitor came to St Columcille at his monastery in exile at Iona in Scotland. The saint asked the mysterious youthful visitor the origins of the lake they were seeing. The visitor answered, 'I know that it was yellow, it was flowery, it was green, it was hilly, it was rich in strewn rushes, and silver, and chariots. I have grazed it when I was a stag: I have swum it when I was a salmon, and when I was a seal; I have run upon it when I was a wolf; I have gone around it when I was a human, I have landed there under three sails: the yellow sail which bears, the green sail which drowns, the red sail under which flesh was conceived. Women have cried out because of me, although father and mother do not know what they bear with labour for living folk, with a covering for the dead.'[16]

Here we have Columcille's other world visitor discussing the elaborate transmigration of his soul.

The druid class served not only as perpetuators of the great Irish myths; as poets they were also the authoritative propagators of the myths, through their disciplined and exacting memories. Druids' roles in the myths approximated their actual roles in early Irish society. They were called upon by their kings to divine or prophesy the outcome of looming battles, to work their magic in helping to destroy the enemy, and to heal the battle-wounded warriors of their people.

James Bonwick says that wherever the druids appeared 'miracles were abundant, as they have been in all periods of Irish history. The deity, the angels, the spirits of the air or elsewhere, are ever at hand to work a marvel ... As the performances of saints are precisely similar to those attributed to druids, one is naturally puzzled to know where one party quits the field and the other comes on.'[17]

Miranda J. Green, who teaches at the University of Wales, describes the rich and varied religious tradition of the Celtic peoples. She states that this 'variety and complexity is due largely to the essential animism which appears to have underpinned the Celtic religion.' She notes that the Celtic people believed 'that every part of the natural world, every feature of the landscape, was numinous, possessed of a spirit ... These natural forces were perceived as capable of doing humankind good or harm, and so they had to be controlled and their power harnessed by means of divination, sacrifice and other propitiatory rituals ... Sacred space could take the form of built shrines, but equally important were natural cult foci such as lakes, springs and trees or open-air enclosures where worshippers were not cut off from the numinous landscape around them.'[18]

One difficulty in assessing the role of druids is that the Church eventually supplanted their religious dimension and throughout most of medieval Ireland possessed a near monopoly on writing and copying documents. The Church sought to ensure that these 'pagan instruments of Satan' were not given much credit regarding their value to society. Yet, through a scrutinous review of the early manuscripts, one can infer some useful information about the druids in Irish society.

P. W. Joyce felt that the most significant component of Ireland's history involved the culture prior to Ireland's invasions by the Vikings, Normans and English. Much of the source material Joyce used in his two-volume classic is derived from ancient manuscripts. He noted that: 'The druids had the reputation of being great magicians: and in this character they figure more frequently and conspicuously than in any other, both in ecclesiastical and in lay literature. So true is this, that the most general Irish word for sorcery, magic, or necromancy, is *druidecht*, which simply means 'druidism' – a word still in use. [Druids] could – as the legends tell – raise druidical clouds and mists, and bring down showers of fire and blood; they could drive a man insane or into idiocy flinging a magic wisp of straw in his face.'[19]

Thomas F. O'Rahilly brilliantly describes the function of the other world and how it was accessed as a source of wisdom.[20] The Celts believed that the other world was the source of all wisdom. The gods of the other world, from which wisdom could be obtained, themselves were able to take many shapes, including the animal shapes of a horse, bull, wolf, eagle, hawk, swan, and salmon, among others. No matter what form the gods of the other world took, they were regarded by early Irish society as old and wise.

Pagan myths indicate that druids, and much of Irish early hagiography suggests that saints, empowered by supernatural forces, were also able to change shapes. Journeys to the other world revealed a structure, which often contained elements similar to the natural world, but frequently found in a more perfect form. In addition to gods and other persons inhabiting the other world who could magically impart various gifts of knowledge, there was also the other world well.

When the word 'well' is used in either ancient Irish mythology or in Irish hagiography or in current day Hiberno-English, it usually means a natural spring out of which flows pure, fresh water. Such springs in Ireland bubble up through rocks just beneath the ground's surface, or flow out of rock cracks or fissures seen on mountainsides and cliffs. Many of such ancient 'wells', once regarded by druids as sacred, are presently venerated by Irish Catholics as holy wells in which healing waters abound.

The well of Segais, also known as Connla's well, was believed to be located beneath the sea in *Tír Tairngire*, the other world. Hazel trees grew around the well and dropped nuts into the water, causing bubbles of mystic inspiration to form on all streams fed by the well. The well of Segais was believed to flow into the Boyne River, whereupon chosen mortals were fortunate enough to discover the hazelnuts and to drink the *imbas*, special wisdom, out of them. Anyone who drank this magical water obtained the seer's gift and became an accomplished *filid*, poet and seer. It was also believed that the well of Segais was the source for all the rivers in Ireland. The *filid* were believed to be able to access other world wells and thereby divine occult knowledge.

One means by which such knowledge was accessed was known as *imbas forosnaí* – the poet-seer chews a raw piece of flesh taken from a just-sacrificed pig, dog or cat, chants an incantation over it and offers this masticated meat to the gods he invokes to reveal the knowledge being sought. The poet-seer then sleeps, and in a dream the knowledge is revealed. The results of this ritual were similar, in effect, to drinking from the well of Segais.

According to the Irish legends, a seer was from time to time consulted regarding who should be chosen as the king of Tara, in County Meath. O'Rahilly describes the occult procedure utilised for such divinations, known as *Tairbfheis* or 'bull-sleep'. A bull was ritually slain and the seer ate its flesh and drank its broth, then laid down to sleep, perhaps wrapped in the bull hide, whereupon the image of the future king appeared to him in a dream.

The Irish secular priest and historian, Geoffrey Keating (1580–1644), wrote a book which would dominate the historic field for the next two centuries, despite its comprehensive inclusion of pseudo-historical material from Irish myths that Keating and others believed to be fact.[21] Keating reported that seekers of occult wisdom would make wattles of the Mountain Ash, then known as the Quicken Tree, 'spread thereon the hides of the bulls offered in sacrifice, putting the side which had been next to the flesh uppermost', thus invoking the other world gods to come and impart knowledge as the seer slept, lying on the meaty side of the bull hide.

A *síd* (pronounced shee) is an underground dwelling place of certain inhabitants of the other world. The people who dwell in the *síd* are known as the *áes síde* or folk of the hollow hills. 'Normally thought of as dwelling beneath the earth or under water, they are portrayed as the guardians of the territories and the ancestors of royal lineages, controlling the weather and the crops, presiding over the practice of the arts and the frenzy of battle.'[22]

One of the *áes síde* appeared to Connla the Red, son of Conn of the Hundred Battles, and told him: 'I come from the lands of living folk where there is no death nor sin nor transgression. We consume everlasting feasts without labour. There is concord among us without strife. It is a great *síd* in which we are, so that because of this we are called *áes síde*.'[23]

Within Irish myths, certain warrior heroes such as Fionn Mac-Cumhail could also access occult knowledge. One day Fionn found the door of a *síd* open. The daughters of the owner of the *síd* tried to deny Fionn and his two companions access to the magic well inside. One daughter, at that moment, was holding a vessel filled with water from the well. In the struggle to close the door, some of the water spilled out of the vessel and into the mouths of Fionn and his companions. As a result of tasting this water the three men acquired *fíos*, the capacity for divine wisdom.

Another belief about Fionn's acquisition of supernatural knowledge and wisdom is associated with his thumb. Again, Fionn and his two companions seek entry to a *síd* but the three daughters of Bec MacBuain shut the door. Each of the daughters holds a cup filled with 'the liquid of inspiration', which is spilled during the fracas. Fionn, upon removing his badly bruised thumb from the doorjamb, puts it in his mouth, tasting the spilled drops of liquid.

Fionn's thumb served him well on more than one occasion. Another time he had caught a magic fish, the salmon of Linn. While cooking it Fionn touched the hot salmon with his thumb, scalding himself. When he put his thumb in his mouth and tasted the salmon, thereafter nothing was unknown to him. By chewing on his thumb and touching his wisdom tooth, Fionn acquired *imbas forosnaí*.

One final method by which Fionn obtained supernatural knowledge was by *teinm laeda*, which O'Rahilly tells us, means literally the chewing the core of a nut. This involved chewing the thumb while simultaneously chanting an incantation. By the use of such a ritual, Fionn was able to implore the gods to impart special wisdom.

The *Táin Bó Cualgne*, the 'Cattle Raid of Cooley' is one of the best-known Irish myths and features the half-man, half-god warrior hero, Cúchulainn. He also acquires special powers to perform supernatural feats, as do other characters in the *Táin*, including the druids. In this myth the druid Muirgen chanted a poem to the gravestone of Fergus. This incantation resulted in a visionary experience for Muirgen: a great mist suddenly formed around him – for the space of three days and nights he could not be found. And the figure of Fergus approached him in fierce majesty, with a head of brown hair, in a green cloak with a red-embroidered hooded tunic, with gold-hilted sword and bronze blunt sandals. Fergus foretold the whole tale of the *Táin*.

The *Táin* involved a battle between the warriors of Ulster

led by Cúchulainn against the army of Queen Medb (pronounced Maeve) of Connacht. Our warrior hero performs many supernatural feats, including the salmon leap which enables him to jump to impossible heights. Cúchulainn, who was wounded by Ferdia, was attended by druid healers who laid magic amulets on his wounds and said spells to stop the 'spurts and spouts of blood'.

There are a number of Irish legends featuring otherworldly aspects of battle. According to Irish myth, the semi-divine *Tuatha Dé Danann* had conquered, and were ruling, Ireland when the Milesians arrived from Spain. The Sons of Mil then spoke the language that would one day be called Irish. These Milesian invaders defeated the *Tuatha Dé Danann* at Telltown and agreed, following their victory, to allow the *Tuatha Dé Danann* to inhabit the *síd*.

Legend suggests that fissures in rocks can be another portal of entry to the *síd*. One other source of access to the other world is the journey to distant islands and places under the waves. Entry to these places is sometimes associated with an invitation delivered to a mortal and is expressed by a female inhabitant of the other world who seductively persuades the seeker to return with her.

The voyage of Bran entailed such an invitation. Bran heard sweet music and fell asleep. When he awoke he found a branch of silver with white blossoms next to him. He took the branch to his royal house and saw standing outside it a woman in strange clothing who sang about a distant isle upheld by four pillars. She described a white silvery plain where dragon stones and crystals drop. Her description was so enticing that Bran accepted her invitation. Embarking upon the voyage, he soon discovered a man riding over the waves in a chariot toward him. This was Manannan, son of Lir, the sea god who sang to Bran about the Land-beneath-the-Waves. Located in this place is a golden-leafed wood with blossom and fruit, where the birds sing sweetly, a stone makes music, and the people are sinless. Bran later arrives at the island of women where he stays for many years, although it seemed like only a year.

The Voyage of Bran contained all the classic elements of an *imram*: a fairy mistress who summoned Bran to the other world; the voyage and the islands; the Land-beneath-the-Waves; the Island of Maidens; the apple tree and fruit-bearing wood; the use of crystal; the musical stone; the birds singing the hours, and the apparent swift passage of time.[24]

One of the best-known Irish myths involves a journey to the other world by Oisín, son of Fionn, who travelled to *Tír na nÓg*, the land of eternal youth. Summoned by Niamh, a fairy queen, he saw the deep sea open before him. He entered a land of cities built on heights, castles, palaces, flowers, a young fawn, and a maid who held a golden apple in her hand.

Not knowing that he had been in *Tír na nÓg* for over three hundred years, Oisín felt increasingly homesick and asked the king and Niamh for the opportunity to visit Ireland. Oisín was told that if he dismounted and touched the ground while in Ireland he could never return to *Tír na nÓg*.

When Oisín arrived in Ireland he saw that a large flagstone had fallen on several people. He reached down from his magic steed to try to lift the stone and he fell to the ground. He instantly withered into a 'helpless, hopeless, blind old man'.

Early Irish saints were also in touch with the other world. The sixth-century saint, Brendan the Navigator, could sense the presence of angels, ghosts and demons:

'One day when they were on the sea, the devil came in an accursed and dreadful form, and settled on the mast in front of Brendan, and none of them saw him save Brendan only. Brendan then asked the devil why he had come before his proper time, that is before the time of the great resurrection, the Day of Judgement? The devil said at once: "To be tortured in the depths of this black dark sea am I come."

'Brendan then asked him: "How so?"

'"Sad is that," said the devil; "no one can see it and survive."

'However, the devil showed Brendan the door of hell, and he saw its pains and misery.'[25]

The saints called upon angels for assistance in time of trouble. 'One time when Coemgen was reciting his hours, he dropped his Psalter into the lake; and great grief and vexation seized him. And the angel said to him: "Do not grieve". Afterwards an otter came to Coemgen bringing the Psalter with him from the bottom of the lake, and not a line or letter was blotted.'[26]

The early Irish saints, not unlike the druids, were also known to change shapes, sometimes from a man to a woman. In one case St Colman grew a pair of breasts in order to nurse his foster children.

Anne Ross has written about the behavioural similarities of druids and early Irish saints: their performance of miracles; their magical powers; and their cunning. She was particularly impressed by the sixth-century Irish saint, Mochuda, who lived at Rahan, County Offaly:

'On a certain day in early springtime there came to tempt him a druid, who said to him, "In the name of your god cause this apple tree branch to produce foliage."

'Mochuda knew that it was in contempt of the divine power that the druid proposed this, and the branch put forth leaves on the instant. The druid demanded, "In the name of your god put blossom on it."

'Mochuda made the sign of the cross over the branch and it blossomed presently. The druid persisted, "What profits blossom without fruit?"

'For the third time Mochuda blessed the branch, and fruit, fully ripe, fell to the earth. The druid picked up an apple off the ground and examining it, he understood it was quite sour, whereupon he objected. "Such miracles as these are worthless, since the fruit is left uneatable."

'Mochuda blessed the apples, and they became as sweet as honey. And in punishment for his opposition the druid was deprived of his eyesight for a year. He went away, at the end of the year he came back to Mochuda and did his penance, whereupon he received his sight back again, and he returned home rejoicing.'[27]

This account shows the survival of paganism in Ireland in the late sixth century, one hundred and fifty years after St Patrick's arrival and several centuries after the Emperor Tiberius issued a decree against the druids and other learned classes in pagan Gaul in the first century. Ross commented, 'Even at this late date Irish druidism offered an alternative belief-system … The constant druidic presence in the orally transmitted sagas demonstrates the original integral role of this order in pagan Irish society; and the huge corpus of nature learning and tradition was dependent in its written form upon the early churchmen, who tried to record as faithfully as possible'. This mixture of the druidic cosmology with that of the early Christian saints survived up through the early twentieth century as can be seen in a collection of prayers for protection, incantations, spells and charms entitled, *Carmina Gadelica*.

There is an integration of pagan myth with tales about early Irish saints who perform druid-like feats: 'The blending of pagan and Christian lore which confronts us in Ireland's legendary history bears witness to a commitment to both traditions: it is because they were convinced that both were true, and both important, that the Irish sought so persistently to reconcile them with one another ... The prophet and poet, transcending the passing ages and matching the truth of things with his own inspired speech, can win the heart of the mysterious world.'[28]

As I seek to evaluate the significance of the other world to the worldview of contemporary Irish people, several possibilities come to mind. Some of these are grounded in historical fact, while others remain the fruits of speculation. That the *Tuatha Dé Danann* inhabited the *síd*, following their defeat by the Sons of Mil,[29] was taught as part of the 'true' history of Ireland, based largely upon Geoffrey Keating's research, by both clerics and lay scholars up into the nineteenth century. Miraculous feats described in pagan myth and the incredible performances of early Irish saints were also then generally regarded as historical fact.

Seers and saints, including Ireland's patron St Patrick, had visions in which they were able to access other world realities. Over the centuries ordinary Irish people had visions, of both saints and fairies as well as other entities. Many Irish people had the second sight. To them the other world was real and accessible. It coexisted and was intertwined with the material world.

John Moriarty, a contemporary Irish poet and philosopher, wrote about the other worldly 'Connla's well', and explained that his father was Connla to him.

'He nourished a way of seeing things in me. He nourished in me a way of being in the world. When my father asked me how I was he didn't only mean how I was in this world, he was asking me how I was in all worlds. Are my feet philosophically fit to walk elsewhere? If you aren't philosophically fit to walk in the other world you aren't philosophically fit to walk in this world. All other worlds and this world are one world ... As a poet and philosopher, I walk the path to Connla's well. It's my task to keep it open.'[30]

Moriarty knows the other world is inhabited by spirit beings from whom he derives his ability to have visions and see the future. He, like the warriors, druids and saints before him, has drunk from the waters of Connla's well. He knows that 'all other worlds and this world are one world'. To dwell in this realm is to be spiritually enriched. John Moriarty and thousands of other living sensitive Irish people like him, metaphorically wear the lenses that enable them to see and hear a monocosmic reality. In addition to the gods, warriors, druids and saints, who else dwells in these realms? At the very least, fairies, ghosts and demons.

Fairies, ghosts, demons and
PISEÓGS

On Saturday 29 May 1999, I opened the *Irish Times* and saw a photograph of my friend Eddie Lenihan who lives in County Clare. In the background of the photograph was a *sceach* (pronounced skee-ak) or fairy tree. Above the picture of Eddie was a headline: 'Fairy bush survives the motorway planners'.

Gordon Deegan, the reporter, opened his story with these words: 'A "SACRED" fairy bush in County Clare will not after all have to be destroyed in the building of a new bypass motorway, much to the relief of those who attach superstitious beliefs to such features of the Irish landscape ... One of the state's best-known folklorists and storytellers, Eddie Lenihan, had warned that the destruction of the fairy thorn tree ... "could result in a misfortune and in some cases death for those travelling the proposed new road".' It was the fairies who would be causing the deaths in retaliation for the destruction of their bush.

A few hours later I was sitting at Eddie's kitchen table listening to what was so important about this fairy bush: it was a rendezvous point for the Kerry fairies on their way to do battle with the Connacht fairies. The Kerry fairies would regroup at the bush and discuss tactics for the battle. From time to time the white blood of the fairies is visible on the grass near the fairy bush. Fairies are pale because their blood is white. The white blood was from those fairies slain in battle.

Eddie continued: 'Disturbing that bush would be as serious a matter as disturbing a graveyard. In every conceivable way the fairies are like us. They go about their business. They have their families, their entertainments, their roadways. It's just that we, in our ignorance, have forgotten that. Just because we don't see these things doesn't mean they're not there. The only thing we respect any more is the fairy fort because it's so highly visible. And, even then, they've just knocked a fairy fort down the road from here.'

To stop the destruction of the fairy bush, Eddie wrote to the county engineer about the fairy bush. 'I got a standard letter which said this is the plan and the plan has to go ahead. So I thought that was the end of it. But soon the newspapers, radio and television took it up and now they're not going to be cutting it down or moving it. They obviously feel that the publicity is more than they can countenance. So they're altering the course of the motorway.'

If I had not known and respected Eddie, I might have thought that he was either entirely insane or that the story was a hoax. Several sane and well-educated Irish people have told me about fairy bushes or fairy paths. One woman said that as a little girl she was taught 'never to deface or harm a whitethorn tree or the fairies would cause us no end of difficulties. When they are full of beautiful white blossoms in May, we'd never think of snipping off a bouquet as the fairies would get us for sure.'

Just south of Kilkenny I saw a fairy tree, the branches of which were filled with ribbons, rags, socks, scarves and other articles of clothing. This was a healing tree where local people come to ask the fairies for a 'cure'.

Does the government pay any attention to protecting fairy bushes and assorted otherworldly things? The answer is yes. Breandán Ó Cíobháin, helped lead a campaign to stop the building of a hotel on a beautiful, unspoiled beach near Ventry, County Kerry. It was not the pristine nature of the beach alone that won the case, but its connection with the legendary Fionn Mac-

Cumhail and his nemesis, Duinn, the king of the world. Duinn's invasion forces reputedly had landed on this beach. They raped and pillaged the people of Ventry because one of Fionn's look-outs had fallen asleep. Ó Cíobháin argued that to build a resort on this beach would have been a sacrilege. Kerry County Council granted permission to build the hotel. But on appeal to *An Bórd Pleanála*, the planning board, the decision was reversed. One of the main reasons given was that the proposed construction 'would seriously injure the visual amenities of the area … It is considered that the proposed development … would have adverse effect on the cultural heritage of the *Gaeltacht* area.'

If the cultural heritage relating to the legendary King Duinn and Fionn MacCumhail deserved protection from the government of Ireland, then it would be consistent to afford the fairies of Kerry and their thorn bush similar protection.

Most Irish farmers are loath to knock or plough under 'fairy forts' or 'fairy rings' (circular mounds often ringed with stone walls) or disturb 'fairy paths' on their land for fear of the fairies' reprisal. A friend told me that her brother-in-law destroyed a fairy fort on his land and soon afterwards his youngest son was killed while crossing a road. Pure coincidence? Not necessarily so. Literature is full of examples of such deadly fairy retaliations.

There are still many Irish people who believe in other-worldly inhabitants and there are quite a few who say they are in communication with them, or at least able to observe and identify such entities.

Banshee, translated literally from the Irish, means woman fairy. The wailing noise they reputedly make is called keening. They keen before the death of someone, usually either the night before, or two or three days before. The banshee often appears as a young woman with long hair or as an old hag. In Ireland the banshee is the type of fairy most often talked about and most frequently encountered.

Patricia Lysaght grew up in County Clare, one of the most fairy-sensitive areas of Ireland. Lysaght documents hundreds of reported manifestations of banshees, so many in fact that she devised a system of sub-classification for the many different types of banshees.[31]

In Ireland, the banshee is known to everyone, although heard by comparatively few and seen by even fewer. Those who have seen or heard the banshee, it is said, are often family members or neighbours of the person who is about to die. The person who dies, reportedly does not see or hear the banshee.

I had my first introduction to the banshee when, in the summer of 1984, I was driving from Clifden, County Galway to Croagh Patrick, County Mayo. Sarah was in the front seat with me and sitting in the backseat were the grandchildren of Irish friends, Martin and Anna, a couple in their eighties. Birdie was twelve. Raymond was eight. Seamus was six.

All of a sudden we spotted a most peculiar rainbow. Instead of arching high into the sky it appeared flat and parallel to the ground, almost pasted onto the side of a nearby mountain. I asked the children if they thought there might be a pot of gold over there by that mountain.

When they told me they didn't believe in all that I countered with, 'So what do you believe in?'

Birdie immediately blurted, 'Banshees! We all do because they are real. When you hear a banshee keening outside at night someone inside the house will be dead by morning.'

This was a most amusing experience for my wife and me until we returned the children to their parents' house, and called next door to see their grandparents.

As I told the story about the rainbow and the banshee, Martin's expression turned sullen and Anna dropped one of her knitting needles. Their daughter later explained that it's bad luck to talk about banshees because if they hear you, they'll come. And if they come, someone's soon going to die.

I thought at the time that all this banshee business was nothing but ignorant superstition.

Eddie Lenihan told me a banshee story he had heard: 'There were three brothers, all great card players. They would go out nearly every night, sometimes playing cards until dawn. One evening, all three brothers were in a card game and two were soon put out of the game. Having no money left, the two walked home. Seán, the third brother, stayed on and eventually won the game. But because it was so late, instead of walking home along the road, he went through the fields. He walked up a stony hill on a moonlit night, only to hear the lonesome cry of a banshee.

'When Seán stopped walking to listen carefully, the keening stopped. But when he resumed walking, the keening also resumed. Seán thought it was his two brothers blackguarding him, so he continued on over the stony hill. Whenever Seán stopped the keening would stop.

'He made his way toward the sound and he saw in the moonlight a person sitting on a stone. He was certain it was one of his brothers, so he crept up and tried to grab the person.

'To his horrible surprise, Seán saw an old woman's face staring at him and she turned and struck his face. Seán felt blood running down his face. Suddenly the old woman disappeared. When Seán got home his mother saw that his cheek was badly bleeding and that he had four finger marks across his face. She dressed his wounds and put him to bed.

'Seán never got up the next day, so his mother called the doctor who came and re-dressed the wounds. Two days later Seán got out of bed and took off the bandage to find the four finger marks had turned to ugly scars. He tried to hide it by growing a grey beard, but the scars showed through his beard. Soon Seán went mad and not long after he died.'

Eddie explained that the moral of the story is never to interfere with a banshee. But in otherworldly Ireland there are other harbingers of death and he told me about another indicator of imminent death. As is often the case, the banshee in a given area will only keen for certain families. So too in the story of the two little blue lights in County Clare – they only appeared for five specific families.

'These two blue lights are to be found near an old graveyard in Crusheen next to the ruins of an Augustinian abbey located on an island in Inchicronan Lake. They are known as the Island Lights. When a person is to die in the vicinity, these two little blue lights arrive at night at the house of the sick person where they hover at the roof or chimney level. When seen, they're taken as a sure sign that someone soon is going to die, usually within a day or two.

'The origins of these two lights, local people assert, go back to the seventeenth century when one night a person rowed out to the abbey to summon a priest to give last rites to a dying woman. The priest sent the person away saying, "She'll be all right. I'll come in the morning." He didn't want to row to the opposite lake shore, and walk to the dying woman's house, and then back again in the middle of the night. The next day when the priest arrived at the house the woman inside had died without ever receiving the last rites. These rites were believed to provide essential protection to the soul of the dying person.

'The blue lights were an eternal punishment for the priest who had failed to administer the last rites. It became the priest's after-life duty to give warning to the descendants of all families living near the abbey whenever someone was about to die. To this day some descendants of these families have noticed two blue lights hovering over the roof of the house in which one of the occupants was soon to die.'

While most sensitives that I have met in Ireland are women, one man seems to possess an extraordinary sensitivity to tuning into otherworldly phenomena. He told me about seeing a strange light shining on the roof of a house in which a person soon thereafter died. He told me that whenever he was walking with another person and passed a house with the strange moon-like light shining on the roof, when there was no moon in the sky, only he, and not the other person, could see it.

'There was a man that died and a few days before he went, I saw a big moon over his house. It wasn't the moon itself because there was no moon in the sky at all that night. It looked like moonlight on the roof. It came and was gone in seconds. Two days later the man living there was no longer alive. And there was another person, a woman who died of cancer. She was a young housewife and just before she died I saw the same moon at night over her house. There was another man I knew who was married only fifteen years, and he got a pain in his chest. He went to the doctor who said, "Go home, you'll be all right." And that very night I saw the same moon over his roof. And wouldn't you know, the next morning he was dead.

'Then another time I saw a neighbour of mine who was a builder. I used to know him well. I was walking at night. It was four in the morning. He was sawing wood. I heard the sound going tick, tick, tick away. He was making something out of timber, like making a door or whatever. Glory be to God, why is a man making a door in the dark at 4 a.m.? Then I saw a light come down from back behind me. It was shining on him. I could see him tipping a board. I watched him pick it up and take it down the road a half a mile to where he was going to be buried at the bottom of the graveyard.

'What I saw when I first heard the ticking was the light that had come down into his house. But when he picked up his board and walked out of the house the light came with him. I saw the man the following day and he wasn't too well. I was about twenty-seven or twenty-eight at the time. I asked my father if he saw something similar on the roof of the man's house. He said he had seen nothing. My father checked the next day and told me the man was all right. But when I saw that light, I knew it was the fairies coming to get him. And two days later your man was dead.'

A banshee, the blue lights and the white light on the roofs are not the only warning signs of death which emanate from otherworldly sources. There have been numerous other omens manifesting as well. The following account was told to me by Cait Ní Lochlainn from County Cork who works as a reporter. She, like others in her trade, is normally quite suspicious about any tale reporting to have its origins in the non-material world.

'My husband's mother was dying in hospital. She was dying for three weeks at this stage and we didn't expect her to last any longer. But one morning we were still in bed – I'd say it was about 7.30 or 8 a.m. – and we were all asleep. My husband and my daughter – who saw her last – were awakened by this absolutely dreadful knocking on the door. My husband got up and went out and there was nobody there. A phone call came through about a half an hour later to say that she had died about the same time they heard the knocking, or just after it.'

Let us turn now to ghosts. One of the otherworldly characteristics of so many Irish is their remarkable sensitivity to ghosts. Nearly every Irish friend of mine has either told me about experiences of someone in his or her family encountering ghosts, or about some ghostly dimension of local lore.[32]

This is a first-hand account as told to me by Breandán Ó Cíobháin: 'In 1951 when I was thirteen years old at a boarding school in Killarney and was sleeping in my third-floor dormitory room sometime during the middle of the night, I woke up to the sound of air rushing – as if bodies were running frantically all over the place while causing abrasive sounds of air striking hard surfaces. I associated this movement of air with soft slippers rushing across the floor and a swishing of long, full skirts. I lay in my bed, petrified, hearing the sound of air all about me.

'Seven of us were sleeping in one large room. The commotion seemed to be coming out from the door to a bathroom which directly overlooked the cemetery of the nearby convent. This rushing of air and commotion persisted for some minutes and then I became aware of the door opening, which led from our floor to a set of stairs leading down.

'From then on, the sounds were different. There was the sound of tumbling and banging and of doors actually slamming. By the time these noises abated, we were all awake and terrified. We asked one another what had just happened. We were terrified and not too much was said. In subsequent days, we discussed the experience at greater length and then we heard that our house was haunted. The tradition is associated with the death of the priest during the time of the Penal Laws in the eighteenth century, here in Ireland.'[33]

Judy McGinn lives in a four-hundred-year-old castle in Mallow, County Cork. She told me about a woman ghost who lives in her castle. Over a dozen houseguests, who had each slept in a particular guest room, reported hearing nocturnal footsteps in the hallway just outside the room. She herself was once awakened by the ghost's footsteps. One guest, who is quite sensitive, reported hearing the same footsteps during the day in the front hall. Each person described the soft footsteps as sounding like the person making them was wearing slippers. Judy's mother-in-law said that she saw a woman in white floating down the back stairs then disappear down a hallway. She also said that whenever she heard the footfalls of the woman ghost she simultaneously smelled an overwhelming scent of spring flowers, like bluebells and lilacs. There is a legend that a woman comes every spring and leaves a basket of bluebells on the castle's doorstep and that apparently people in past generations had reported seeing the woman leaving flowers on the steps. Early in the twentieth century the lady of the castle had a son who was killed in London. Perhaps she is still looking for him, Judy suggests.

A somewhat similar story was told to me by my friend, Sonia, a sensitive from County Clare. Years ago, she worked in a hotel in County Wicklow. After work, Sonia would return to her room on the top floor of a nearby house. One night she woke up to 'a terrible crying sound' coming from the direction of her balcony. When she walked out onto the balcony to investigate, Sonia heard 'this terrible, heartbroken crying sound coming from the room'. When she returned to the room the sound once again was heard coming from outside. It was 'the crying of a woman in terrible distress. I made discreet enquiries in the hotel the next day but no one heard anything. About a month later I heard a story that a young girl working in the castle nearby had got into trouble by the young lord of the manor and had killed herself and the baby. It was said that on certain nights she took the form of a bird and flew around the top of the hotel weeping and crying for her misfortune and her lost baby.'

Still another friend, Kate, told me about her experience of communicating with her dead grandmother. She also told me about being visited by the ghost of a friend who died of cancer a few years ago: 'I get this smell of gardenias then I know my maternal grandmother is present. Shortly after she died I heard her voice tell me, "I will always walk with you". You get these things when you need them. So often when I need it, she comes. I smell the gardenias.

'My friend Sheila, who died about four years ago of cancer, and I were very close. If I ever had a soul mate, it was Sheila. More often than not I feel her as if she puts her hand on my shoulder. She also knocks in the kitchen on my wooden shelves and upstairs on the wooden doors. Sometimes when I'm not certain that it is Sheila, I say to her, "If that's you Sheila, do it again". And usually she knocks again. One time a medium I was visiting in London, right out of the blue, said, "I have a message for you from a lady. She's telling me to say to you – you are right and I'm very happy". She was referring to a conversation we had as Sheila was dying when she said, "I wish I had your conviction about life after death".

I replied, "I tell you what; if I am right you come and tell me. And if I don't hear from you, I will know that you were right".'

Kate told me 'I believe in the existence of spirits. I believe in the afterlife. I am prepared to and delighted to be in touch with spirits and to be helped by them as well as being sufficiently sensitive to be receptive to their presence. I cannot tune into spirits at will. They tune into me and make themselves known to me. I am very careful about what I do in these realms. So I use prayer in order to keep it on the highest level.'

Therese O'Mahony is a folk healer in County Cork. Her second sight allows her to see ghosts. She has a sister Ethne, whose friend Mary's father died. Therese phoned Mary to express her condolences on Ethne's behalf as she was away. During the conversation, Therese looked over her shoulder and saw 'Mary's father standing behind her, with his head stooped toward the phone, as if he were listening in on the conversation. [His] clothes and cap appeared brighter and more spruce than previously, and his face seemed paler. As he stood there, his fingers were curled up and holding on to the end of the cuff of his coat sleeve.' Mary later confirmed that in real life, her father did indeed regularly grasp his coat sleeve cuffs the way Therese had described.

Therese also said that a few years ago she noticed a woman in eighteenth-century clothing walking across a field, carrying a blue bottle in her hand. Over several days Therese observed that the woman would normally appear at a certain point in the field, then disappear at another location. The woman looked so real that Therese was uncertain whether she was living or disincarnate. One day the woman came to a stone wall, floated up into the air and over the wall and slowly landed on the other side. 'That's when I knew she was a spirit being. She was trying to tell me something. So one day I took my shovel to where she first appeared and I started digging carefully. I discovered her collection of blue bottles. There were nearly one hundred of them.' Therese now displays these bottles on a shelf near the window of her museum.

A scholarly friend told me that the Irish are much more sophisticated than the English when it comes to dealing with ghosts. 'The English tend to associate ghosts with haunted houses and scary things, while the Irish recognise that ghosts are a normal part of the other world. Ghosts usually go about their business in an unthreatening way to humans. The Irish, from the earliest beginnings of their civilisation, recognised that they live in two worlds at once, not only in one world. We are speaking of a monocosmic as contrasted with a bicosmic mentality.'

The Irish poet, William Butler Yeats, spent quite a bit of time with sensitive women during his explorations of otherworldly phenomena.[34] Mary Battle, a servant of Yeats' uncle, had a remarkable ability to tune into otherworldly phenomena and to see into the future. One morning she was bringing his uncle a clean shirt to wear, when she thought she saw blood on it. She brought him another shirt, and that very morning Yeats' uncle fell over a wall and cut himself, bleeding into the shirt in the same place Mary had earlier noticed blood.

Yeats' uncle, on the spur of the moment, would invite a person to come home with him for dinner. Battle often sensed that a guest would be coming and, before Yeats' uncle and his guest arrived, would have set an extra place at the table.

Yeats and one of his colleagues did experiments involving telepathically sending thoughts to Mary as she slept at night. The next day she would invariably report having dreams about the same themes.

Mary Battle's access to otherworldly phenomena included apparitions of Irish mythological persons. One day while staring out the window she saw Queen Medb, leader of the army of Connacht. Mary, in describing the presence of Medb, told Yeats that she was 'the finest woman you ever saw, travelling right across from the mountains and straight to here. She looked very strong but not wicked … She had no stomach on her at all but was slight and broad in the shoulders, and was handsomer than anyone you ever saw; she looked about thirty.' Mary also reported on the entourage from the *síd* travelling with Medb: 'They are fine and dashing looking, like men one sees riding their horses in twos and threes on the slopes of mountains with their swords swinging. There is no such race living now, none so finely proportioned.'

Breandán Ó Cíobháin has talked to hundreds of old-timers about fairy legends and place names, including a woman in the village of Ventry, where he also lives:

'Exactly forty years ago when I was a young college student, I started collecting folklore from an old lady who lived up that mountainside you see over there. I used to go up to her in the winter evenings on my bike and transcribe in long hand, word for word, what she said. There were no tape recorders available then. I published the text of one of the tales she told which was fascinating. But she herself had something very special about her. How I got to know her was that my father had a shop and she would come down the mountain to do her shopping at his shop.

'She had been married three times. The first husband was drowned in a fishing accident. The second was drowned in a similar situation. She had gone to live then with relatives of hers. She used to tell me every night that she was quite happy to tell me the tales, but that it broke her heart that I was interfering with her prayers and her communications with the other world.

'She would sit down with her rosaries at night and she said she spent all night praying. She dressed in black and had a long string of rosary beads hanging down from her waist. That was not unusual; that was back when many people had rosaries and prayed a lot. But one evening she gave me an insight into her mentality, which I suppose she wouldn't have given to most people.

'She told me that when she lay in bed at night on most nights she could see through a little window on the gable end of the house. From that perspective she had a clear view of the mountainside. Before I tell you what she said you should know that I grew up in an era when fairies were considered to be an everyday reality, not a cultural relic of the past. She told me how each night she saw this wonderful, fantastic procession of fairies, surrounded by bright lights, come down the mountainside making sort of a humming noise and pass by on the way to the bottom of the mountain. The term that is used in folklore for this phenomenon is *An Slua*, which means the host or hosting. I questioned her then if she was sure she was not dreaming. "No," she said, "I am absolutely awake." This was something she was experiencing wide-awake and that was a dimension that was revealing itself to her. Even though she was a *seanchaí*, it was not one of the stories she had memorised that she was telling me, but a part of her daily life, things she had seen, had heard and that were very real to her.

'She said that seeing *An Slua* happened regularly to her. When she said she was praying all night, I realise that for her it was participating in a reality. It was a different world from the one I was inhabiting, but, still the same, quite real and part of her normal consciousness. She didn't lapse into this world at certain times and live out of it the rest of the time. She lived in both worlds simultaneously. To us the world of the fairies would be quite extraordinary, but to her, it was all one reality, part and parcel of everyday life.'

A Kerry farmer told me that one time he saw a 'man who lived twelve miles away looking for his dog. Soon after, I'll tell you, one morning I got up and heard there was a dog killing sheep – a lonely dog that used to come by at night and kill a sheep and be gone in the morning. Every dog like that would come in the dark and be gone by dawn. It was then that I was mowing hay in the month of June. I saw the first sheep killed. I went up the following day to see what he'd done to the sheep. Another sheep was dead and the dog had gone home. I sent my sheepdogs after him. My dogs found his scent and trailed him, but I didn't follow after because they could have picked up the scent of another dog and I didn't want to be killing the wrong dog. On the third day I went up again and found the third sheep killed by the dog.

'So that night I went after him with my gun and my two good dogs. I went up at 11 p.m. and waited and waited. 1 a.m. came. 2 a.m. came. And 3 a.m. came. I was hopin' the dog would come, but I didn't see a trace of him.

'Then all of a sudden I heard a call and then I saw a white object. What the heck is that? I thought to myself. Before I sat down with the two dogs to wait, I set down two bottles of milk and some food on a rock about eight steps from where I was sitting with my two dogs lying beside me. And didn't that white thing come down and jingle the two bottles together. It was a white fairy with a little light that did it. He was about five-eight or five-nine. He had a white face and was wearing a white gown and he dinged the two bottles together, he did, to show that he was there. He faced me and I couldn't find the gun, my hands were shaking so hard. The heat of the dogs so near me kept me warm. They were very affectionate and would stay close to me. They were soon leaning up against me shaking like a leaf after they saw the fairy. If I tried to point the gun at him maybe I could scare him away, but my own hands were shaking too much to even find the gun in the dark.

'The fairy took two steps away from the food after he clinked the two bottles together. Then he came toward me. Then he turned and when he had gone about fifty yards away he said, "go" or "go home" or "you should be at home". I was not going to argue, so I went home straight away.

'My father asked if I got anything. I said no and went to bed.

Then at 4.30 a.m. I woke up and had a vision of the fairy. It was the same fairy standing there next to my bed. He told me that the dog had come and named the exact place where the killer dog was. So I put on my clothes, got my dogs and gun and went to where the fairy said, and I saw a dog there killing a sheep and shot it just at the dawn of the day. After that, no dog ever killed a sheep in the area for the next ten years. The good people were helping us, sure. It looks like a dream. But it was the real thing.'

Sometimes the good people can help you, but not always. Most Irish country people who respect the fairies would never pick a fight with one or intentionally cause a fairy any harm. Fairies are both respected and feared. To harm an otherworldly creature is highly inadvisable.

Mollie McMahon was born in Querrin, County Clare in 1905 and died in 1990. In her autobiography she talks about the fairies:

'There used to be stories about our [fairy] forts, especially the small one. Dad used to believe them. One was about his grandmother Peg (O'Brien) McMahon. She knew this old lady well, I think she was Hedderman, at least she was an aunt to Martin Hedderman, that I knew in my time. She was walking about the fort and she was taken in by the fairies and kept there by them until she became a very ugly old woman.

'There was a friend of hers in the fort also and he told her what ever she do, not to take any food there. But she must have done it. When she got a chance to run out of the fort she did and they [the fairies] pelted her with sods and one stuck in her back and left her with a breast in the back the same as the front.

'Another old woman told me in her parents' time that two girls were working with corn or hay near the fort and they heard the grandest music there. One girl was very frightened and ran home and into bed. The other one caught up her skirt and danced to the music and nothing happened to her. But the one who ran home never again got out of bed. She died in a few days.'

That the fairies often desire human companionship is a recurring element in Irish folklore. As a general rule, when companionship of a human is sought by the fairies and generously given, there will be no resulting punishment. But when it is refused, the price is often sickness or death. In some stories the fairies abduct a person for a period of time ranging from a few years to an entire lifetime. In others, the fairies seem to want human company for only an hour or so.

Mollie McMahon also wrote about a secret entrance at the side of the fairy fort through which one could gain entrance to a cavern beneath where gold was supposedly stored. She said that a neighbour of theirs spent hours digging a hole hoping to find the secret entrance, but never succeeded.

Medieval Irish myths and legends commonly referred to otherworldly realms of devils and demons.[35] Certainly the story of Brendan the Navigator contains explicit reference to a meeting with Satan. A Kerry farmer told me about his first-hand encounter in coming face-to-face with the Devil:

'There was this man who was nearly eighty-eight years old and he got sick. I was sent to the house by my father to spend the night with him and his family. At 1 a.m. there came this desperate storm. Then this thing came to the shed on the way up to the house. It belted the shed. It belted the gate. It belted the house. It was the door he was belting. You'd think the house was falling. The poor craythur. It seemed he was going to die.

'When the old man heard the noise outside he screamed. He was then inside his room. I was sitting at the fire with three more of the family. I wanted to get to the bottom of all this dreadful belting going on. The beating and noise had been lasting for several minutes. "Glory," I said, "what's happening out there?" But they wouldn't let me step outside.

'Then he came again the second night. I was sent back again and once more I heard the belting. Who was making all the noise? We thought it must be the Devil himself. The whole family heard the noise. The very same thing happened again the second night. It came at 1 a.m. He was hitting the shed again and belting the gate. He was banging on the door.

'The old man upstairs screamed and shouted. "He came again. He came again tonight." He started the screeching because something upset him. That was the Devil, sure. Did he ever see him? I don't know, but you could hear the man screeching from a mile away. He shouted at the Devil, "Go away! Go away! Stop!"

'I was asked back the third time to stay the night because the old man was dying. It was 1 a.m. again. I was standing in the living-room with the young man of the house. And I heard this chain outside. We were ploughing together many years. The old man had a mare and my father had a stallion. When the mare would be in season I'd chain the stallion so he'd stay at home and not go over to bother the mare.

'So there I was with the young man of the house and didn't I hear the chain banging against the road below. I thought the horse had taken the way around from up above to come over to the mare. I had tethered the horse so he could not go anywhere very fast with the chain that was fastened with leather around his front legs. So when the horse moved, the chain would clang against the road. I heard the banging of the chain out by the gate and I thought the horse would damage the gate outside the house so I went outside with the young man and said, "I'll find my horse now."

'There was a field next to the gable of the house and I heard the chain there. I looked around the side of the house and there was nothing there. Then I heard the noise on the other side, so I went back to look for the horse there. I saw nothing. I heard it clang against the gate again. But there was nothing there. So I walked down past the gate over to the ditch to see if it was there. And I saw the Devil there. I saw the face of a man with two horns sticking up out of his forehead. He had two *crubeens* for hands – that's goat's hoofs he had for hands. He stared at me with a fierce horrible look on his face, like he was saying, "Go away! Get out of here!" But he didn't say anything.

'He just stood there cradling a skull under his left arm next to his chest. He made no move. So I ran to look for the young man who went out with me. I don't know if he was listening to the clanging of the chains. I was running around not knowing whether to keep looking for my horse or to run back inside. The gate was nearly all torn up from the belting with the chain.

'Your man inside the house – maybe the window was open – he must have heard the chains. Then came his screaming from inside again. He was shouting, "He came again tonight! He came again tonight! Go away! Go away! Leave me alone! Scare him away! Help me!" Then I ran back inside and asked the old man if he was all right. I never told him what I saw. He died shortly after that.'

Although the farmer was telling me a story that happened about forty-five years ago, by the way he was describing his experience, you would have thought it had happened yesterday. He crossed himself when he finished the story and told me that ever since he's been going to Mass two or three times a week.

The Lives of Irish Saints contains many instances of these holy men uttering horrible curses on those who defied them. The druids did it before them. My friend John Moriarty told me that he experienced such evil-intending behaviour in his own lifetime. In Ireland such necromancy is referred to as *piseóg* (pronounced pishogue):

'One day opening a wyand of hay in the west field, my father found four bad eggs at the heart of it. This, as it would to any neighbour for miles around, brought the cold sweat out through him. But he had to stand his ground. He had to deal with the evil, because this was *piseóg*, a kind of witchcraft, certainly something more wicked then mere superstition. Settling a bed of hay on the four prongs of his fork, he took the eggs, praying as he did so, and laid them on it. Then, careful that no egg would fall off, he walked towards the river. And the river, he was so glad to tell us when he came home, had taken the awful thing out of our land. Only slightly degenerated from its Neolithic enormities, this kind of witchcraft was as common to our locality as its bushes were. No year went by but some awful new story did the rounds. One story had it that a woman opened her door one morning and a skinned calf fell inwards across her threshold. Another story had it that a priest who openly confronted the evil had, within a week, been confronted by it, in truly sensational form, within his own church.

'Dimly, we were aware that this form of witchcraft was based on the belief that like creates like. The bad eggs or the bad butter or the bad meat that someone placed in a field would turn the cattle that grazed that field into its image and likeness. Before long those cattle would themselves be bad meat. In other words, this didn't work by the physical transmission of physical bacteria. It worked by the ritual power of sympathetic magic.'

Another person I know told me about an elderly woman in the west of Ireland who believed that a curse had been placed on her animals. To counteract the curse she hung mirrors on the outside of her animal stalls to deflect the evil energy being sent her way. The mirrors, she believed, would send a malign energy back to the person who had put the curse on her.

St Gobnait, a sixth-century Irish woman, was reputed to have many powers. She was an excellent beekeeper, an extraordinary healer and she had the power to send destructive evil energy at her enemies by throwing a perfectly round, cannon ball-shaped rock at them. It would kill them or destroy their houses and then return to her. The ball was kept at the ruin of her church in Ballyvourney, County Cork. Until a few years ago people would come to the church ruin and borrow the stone ball to take home long enough to use it to put a curse on someone they didn't like. Then the parish priest arranged to have St Gobnait's destructive stone ball permanently cemented into the ruin of the church to stop the parishioners using it to put curses on people.

At the grave of St Gobnait, near the ruined church, is a Bullaun stone, with a hemispherical cavity carved into it so that it can act as a receptacle for rainwater. The pools of raindrops which accumulate in the hollowed indentations in these stones, are believed to possess magical powers capable of doing both good and evil. Pilgrims to St Gobnait's shrine sometimes dip their fingers into the rain-filled cavity of the Bullaun stone, cross themselves and say prayers while walking clockwise around the grave. There are Bullaun stones next to many ancient Irish saints' graves. Most people who make their pilgrimages to such graves often walk reverently in a clockwise circle around the burial place of the long dead saint. But those who may want to curse their enemies reportedly walk around the saint's grave in a counter clockwise-direction.

From these predominantly first-hand experiences and the lore that shrouds them we can discern that there are still quite a few Irish people connected to otherworldly phenomena. Some are sensitives who seem merely to observe otherworldly activities. Others work with otherworldly entities in the hope of achieving good. For still others the intention seems not to be so benevolent.

Nowadays attention is focused away from otherworldly matters onto more material matters and less attention is being paid to fairies, ghosts, second-sighted healers, demons and *piseógs*. Nevertheless, thousands of Irish people in rural parts of the country somehow manage to stay connected to these otherworldly beings.

SAINTS AND ANGELS

The journey to the other world known as an *imram* was just one type of encounter with the other world. Ever since Jesus took to the desert for forty days and the third-century desert fathers followed suit to draw closer to God, Christians have had their own template for their *imrams* to the other world.

The common name for such a journey, as it has evolved over the centuries, is pilgrimage. A pilgrim is one who journeys to a holy place in the hope of experiencing a divine encounter. This can take many forms, including seeing the divine, hearing the divine, apparitions of heavenly beings, miracle cures and many other experiences.

In Ireland there were sacred places before St Patrick ever arrived. These consisted of holy wells, stone circles, graves, megaliths, oak groves and cult sites. The druids would walk worshipfully in a clockwise direction around these sites, uttering incantations and conducting various rituals. When they walked counter clockwise, the druids were engaged in sending curses. The Church tried to stop all such practices, but the people tenaciously returned to such sites, so the Church 'Christianised' them, by requiring the pilgrims to make the sign of the cross, say

Christian prayers and inscribe crosses on the stones they circled. The Church encouraged using the clockwise direction, forgetting the fact that early Christian saints in Ireland put curses on their enemies just as the druids had done.

To this very day thousands of Irish pilgrims journey to sacred places each year, in Ireland or abroad.[36] Some of the favourite places abroad, in addition to the Holy Land, include Medjugorje, Fatima and Lourdes (sites of Marian apparitions), and locations associated with the saints: Theresa of Liseux, Francis, Martin, Anne, Ignatius of Loyola and Padre Pio, among others. These saintly characters often appear in visions to some of the Irish pilgrims who visit such sites.

Within Ireland pilgrims attend the shrine at Knock, County Mayo (site of a Marian apparition on 21 August 1879); St Patrick's Purgatory on an island in Lough Derg, County Donegal (where fasting and praying without sleep are practised); and Croagh Patrick, a rocky desolate mountain in County Mayo where Patrick allegedly spent forty days, which thousands of pilgrims climb on the last Sunday in July. Before the Church changed the date to the last Sunday in July the pilgrims would make the same climb in early August to worship the Celtic god Lugh. These are the best known sites, and pilgrims attending these are usually closely supervised by the Church.

There are many sites that are not so closely supervised by the Church including graves of early Christian saints, holy wells, grave stones, Bullaun stones, standing stones, or healing trees (sometimes referred to as Fairy Bushes).

More recently established holy places in Ireland are the sites of Marian apparitions which have inspired the construction of grottos, often patterned after the Lourdes model. Mary, also known as Our Lady or the Blessed Virgin Mother, stands in front of a cave or grotto. To Mary's right is kneeling St Bernadette Soubirous (the fourteen-year-old French girl who had an apparition at Lourdes in 1858 at which Our Lady said, 'I am the Immaculate Conception'). Near the site is located a holy well from which pilgrims drink the water. Often such grottos are built because, in an apparition, Our Lady requested that a grotto be built.

Pilgrims visit those sites and say decades of the Rosary, or offer prayers to Our Lady or her Divine Son such as St Faustina's Divine Mercy Prayer, the Memorare, the Prayer to the Sacred

Heart and the Brown Scapular.

In 1985 in Ballinspittle, a little West Cork village, the statue of Our Lady at a grotto apparently began to move. Word of this extraordinary phenomenon started to spread. Soon bus loads of pilgrims were arriving there in hopes of encountering an apparition of Our Lady.

I interviewed a number of women who had experienced Marian apparitions. They refer to themselves as visionaries and although each of their apparitional experiences was uniquely their own, a pattern emerged regarding how they began to experience and react to such apparitions. Some saw only Our Lady, but did not hear her speak, whereas others stated that they received specific messages of love, or general spiritual exhortations to pray.

Most of the women also had visions of Jesus, nearly always in the company of His Mother. Four of the women reported having apparitions of the Blessed Virgin Mother and her Son at various locations, sometimes at a number of grottoes, sometimes elsewhere, such as in their homes.

The visionaries, as well as witnesses who observed them during the time they were experiencing the apparitions, reported behaviour associated with deep trance states (i.e., difficulties in breathing, fixed staring at the subject of the vision and oblivious to the immediate material environment, except for sensing the vision), and sometimes they would appear more relaxed and aware of both the vision and what was going on around them.

Each one believes that what they term 'apparition', is more than a vision and is an actual appearance. They also tend to believe that it is not any inherent capacity on their part that enables them to have visions, but that they were chosen by Our Lady or Our Lord to witness such appearances.

The apparitions experienced at the grotto occurred during, or immediately after, praying. These prayers are recited quickly and repetitiously in unison, with a definite cadence, which prevents the mind from wandering. Their prayerful utterances often sound mantra-like.

Most experienced a desire or inner guidance directing them to go to a particular grotto. They would go to a grotto and kneel in prayer, reciting the Rosary and other prayers to Our Lady. The first apparition usually took the form of the face on the statue of

Our Lady becoming lifelike, with the eyes moving and then looking down, and the lips smiling. The visionaries experienced initial doubt and suspected the vision either had not taken place or was imagined. They felt a deep love coming from Our Lady, directed at them, and a sense of calmness, peace and beauty.

One visionary indicated that she had her first Marian apparition in her home:

'When Our Lady first visited me, it was in early December of 1994, about a month after I had met my Guardian Angel. I was at home, awake, sitting on the edge of my bed, and I saw rays of light and saw and smelled roses. Then Our Lady appeared in the rays, standing there in the light just looking at me. I couldn't stop staring at her and didn't know at the time who she was. She wore blue and white and was very beautiful. She looked as if she were a sixteen-year-old girl. She just looked at me and it felt like she was watching me in a loving way. She didn't say a word. It lasted, I guess, for about five minutes.'

Following the initial apparition, the visionaries felt a sense of loss or sadness. They also felt that they were not worthy of the apparition.

During the next apparition the visionaries experienced Our Lady as replacing the statue, appearing as a beautiful, young girl with radiant smile and loving eyes, clothed in garments traditionally associated with Marian dress, surrounded by a glowing light.

In later apparitions, Our Lady would sometimes be recognised as Our Lady of Fatima or Lourdes. She may switch from the Fatima to the Lourdes image, or *vice versa*, and then, more rarely, her vestments would turn to a peach or golden colour. The visionaries generally were highly attentive to the dress and appearance of both Our Lady and Our Lord.

After a few apparitions of Our Lady were experienced at the grotto, the visionaries were often introduced to her Divine Son.

One described her vision as follows:

'Jesus was about six feet tall. He was very, very strong and looked like he was thirty-odd. He was very handsome. His hair is always middle-creased and it's shoulder length, just below his shoulders, wavy and curly at the ends, brown-black. He's got a trimmed beard. Sometimes you see photographs of Jesus with dimples, but he really doesn't have dimples. His beard is just lovely and trimmed. His eyes are brown and his skin is sallow. He had a long nose and nice eyebrows, not very bushy or anything.'

In some cases, individual visionaries would receive spoken messages of greetings and love or be given specific instructions. For example, three of the visionaries received individual specific instructions to build a grotto in honour of Our Lady, and one reported being instructed to build a House of Prayer in County Limerick.

At other times, some of the visionaries reported having apparitions of various saints, most often Padre Pio, who reportedly would occasionally leave the scent of roses; others included St Anne, Bernadette of Lourdes, Francesca of Fatima, Ignatius of Loyola, John of the Cross, Patrick, Theresa of Liseux, angels and apostles.

One who saw a vision of John of the Cross reported:

'I saw St John of the Cross in my house. About six years ago my sister was dying of cancer. I used to go visit her every day in hospital in Cork city. I was very tired because of all the long hours every day visiting my sister in hospital. One morning I was very tired when I got up to go to the bathroom before leaving to see her. As I turned around to head toward the basin a man stood in front of me and he was shorter than I, and he was thin, and he had a priest's habit, and he had a crucifix about nine inches long in his hand, and he had it caught toward his chest.

He had soft curly hair cut in a round. He said to me, 'I'm St John of the Cross. I'll help you.' Then he disappeared. Shortly after that my sister died and when I was at her funeral I was in a trance and could sense that she was with God.'

A visionary who had a vision of the apostles indicated:

'About four years ago, after several Rosaries, I looked up and saw two figures in white robes, about six feet tall and very strong, who looked like the apostles. They had white cords around their waists. They seemed to be running in slow motion at the back of the statue. They were running through the air. They ran around in the air for about two minutes. When the people in white had left, I talked to a man at the grotto who said it was angels we saw. I told him no, it was apostles, because angels don't wear cords around their waists.'

Four of the visionaries reported apparitions similar to those

180

associated with Fatima or Medjugorje, of the sun spinning down and illuminating the grotto in multi-coloured shining rays.

One reported that she had seen 'the sun coming out from behind a cloud and the sun left the sky like it did in Fatima and came down on the grotto and it stayed for a few seconds and time stood still. It was spinning out beautiful colours. Then three amber clouds came out of the spinning sun and one went over a hawthorn tree and the whole hawthorn tree glowed. Another amber cloud went over to the crucifix down the road and it circled the crucifix and all the colours of the rainbow circled the crucifix. The third cloud stayed over the grotto.'

Another saw the Sacred Heart. Three of the visionaries reported what could be classified as pre-cognitive viewing, possibly associated with out-of-body trips, in which the visionary would be shown an event in a distant location, which was either taking place contemporaneously or would occur at a future date. Two of the visionaries reported being taken by Our Lady and Our Lord on a tour of Heaven, Purgatory and Hell.

Several of the visionaries had experiences associated with healing. One, who for the past twelve years had been immobile and confined to a wheelchair, reported an angel coming one day and taking her pain away. She reported on three other occasions being led by Jesus to drink holy water, then getting up out of her wheelchair and walking. The woman said her angel explained that these walking experiences were sent as 'signs' and she was not meant to be fully 'cured' because she was meant to be a 'victim soul' and that her suffering would benefit others.

Her guardian angel wakes her up every morning about 5 a.m., to pray and to give her instructions. Her husband reported that if he is already awake when the angel comes, he is able to see the flesh on her wrist being depressed as if some invisible fingers are gently squeezing her.

Sometimes St Faustina appears and speaks through her to her husband. He said, 'She is usually saying a prayer. Then she goes into a deep sleep, then St Faustina starts speaking through my wife with a heavy Polish accent. She tells me about my wife's work, explains her stigmata and how her suffering as a victim soul is helping people in Purgatory. She also gives me words of encouragement and tells me to keep looking after my wife and be patient with her. She answers any questions I have and so on.

Then sometime later my wife awakens and she doesn't remember anything about St Faustina. She just says she's been away praying with the angels or that she's been in a monastery praying with the monks.'

All these visionaries report that their apparitions have brought them, and usually their family and some of their friends, closer to Our Lady and Our Lord. All attend Mass at least once a week, and several do so daily.

All feel that their apparitions have shaped their lives and given them a highly focused purpose in life. Several of the visionaries have set aside a room in each of their respective homes, to be used for prayer where they conduct regular prayer sessions for their families, neighbours and friends.

If other world sensitivity is indigenous to Ireland, then these Irish visionaries are as likely to be seeing Our Lady, her Divine Son, apostles, saints and angels, just as others reportedly see fairies, ghosts and demons.

The women's descriptions of their experiences suggest mystical qualities of ineffability, noetic quality, transiency and passivity. There is also a positive basis of comparison between the descriptions of the Irish visions and the mystical insights experienced and reported by Teresa of Avila, Ignatius of Loyola, and John of the Cross.

William James, a nineteenth century Irish-American scholar, who wrote a classic text on the psychology of spiritual experiences, believed that 'mystical states, when well developed, usually are, and have the right to be, absolutely authoritative over the individual to whom they come.'[37] That their visions could be authoritative may have also been strengthened when several who prayed together at the grotto would meet afterwards to confirm that they were each seeing the same vision. Furthermore, such experiences also seemed to have had the additional value to those Irish women, of feeling deeply loved by the Blessed Virgin Mother, by Jesus, by the saints and the angels, which resulted in a strengthening of their commitment to their faith, to caring for others, and to enduring sometimes devastating hardships.

James observed, 'When in addition to these phenomena of inspiration, we take religious mysticism into account, when we recall the striking and sudden unifications of a discordant self which we saw in conversion, and when we review the extravagant obsessions of tenderness, purity and self-severity met with in saintliness, we cannot, I think, avoid the conclusion that in religion we have a department of human nature with unusually close relations to the transmarginal or subliminal region.' Quite clearly the content of the descriptions of the Irish visionaries' apparitional experiences falls close to, if not in the centre of, the transmarginal or subliminal realm.

The religious experience of prayer can give rise to a profound awareness of a connectedness to the divine – 'in the consciousness which individuals have of an intercourse between themselves and higher powers with which they feel themselves to be related. This intercourse is realised at the time as being both active and mutual ... Something is transacting.' A person 'becomes conscious that his higher part is conterminous and continuous with a MORE of the same quality, which is operative in the universe outside of him, and which he can keep in working touch with, and in a fashion get on board and save himself when all his lower being has gone to pieces in the wreck.' The visionaries feel that they are in communion with the divine, not only when they pray, but while experiencing each apparition.

James stresses the very real extent to which neurological conditioning affects a person's attitude and orientation to religious experience. This also seems to apply to the nature of the apparitions experienced by the Irish Catholic visionary women whom I interviewed. They experienced visions of Mary, Jesus, the Holy Spirit as dove, saints and angels, all of whom are well established characters in the hierarchical pantheon of Roman Catholic spirit beings. None of the apparitions seemed to contradict the traditional teachings of the Church. Rather, they tended to conform to such teachings as had likely been communicated to the visionaries since their infancy.

One additional value, which the visionaries' example could enhance, seemed to be touched upon by James when he wrote: 'When a religion has become an orthodoxy, its day of inwardness is over: the spring is dry; the faithful live at second hand exclusively and stone the prophets in their turn. The new Church, in spite of whatever human goodness it may foster, can be counted upon as a staunch ally in every attempt to stifle the spontaneous religious spirit, and to stop all later bubblings of the fountain from which in purer days it drew its own supply of inspiration.'

My discussions with several priests revealed some criticism of the visionaries. In fact, the local bishop sought to shut down the House of Prayer in Achill until its visionary founder, Christina Gallagher, would agree to subordinate her operations, and turn over contributions received, to the Church. She refused to knuckle under. More than one priest suggested that such apparitions are the work of the devil. Some priests ignore the fact that the visionaries were having apparitions. There is the rare courageous priest who serves as spiritual director to a visionary seeking clerical support.

The grottos at which most visionaries pray are not maintained by the Church, but usually by devout lay people. The visionaries don't ask the priest's permission to pray in the grottos. They feel drawn to do so on their own. They individually intend to deepen their devotion, the mystical fruits of which have so remarkably enriched their lives. Their humility is as pure as their connectedness to the Divine is deep. For each of them their soul is central to their identity, life's purpose and being. Their dedication to responding obediently to the divine commands is an impressive expression of their faith. Yet their faith is based primarily upon what they see and hear in their visions, rather than upon abstract theological concepts.

It does not come as a surprise that in Ireland many people still thrive in a monocosmic reality. How many portals are there in Ireland through which to enter the other world? I suspect there are many I have not yet encountered. But I know of one additional portal in which the participants, often to their delight, are able to tune into the other world.

IN TUNE WITH THE OTHER WORLD
— THE RAPTURE OF MUSIC

Musical talent is such a rich part of the Irish gene pool that virtually every person born in Ireland has a love of music. Music and dance are so endemic to Irish culture that whenever you attend a local rural community celebration, you are likely to find a group of children performing on the accordion, tin whistle, fiddle, banjo, guitar, uilleann pipes, flute, piccolo or *bodhrán* (pronounced bow-raun; a tambourine-shaped drum). Nearly every little girl in rural Ireland is fitted out with dancing shoes and an elaborately designed dancing dress for performing traditional Irish step dancing which is often seen at rural parish halls, community centres or local fairs.

The parents often engage in set dancing at a *céilí* (pronounced kay-lee), an organised evening of dancing, usually accompanied by a *céilí* band. Afterwards the people will often adjourn to a local pub featuring Irish traditional musicians performing jigs, reels and other such tunes.

But the power of Irish music resounds far beyond the walls of local pubs. Ireland has won more awards in the annual Eurovision Song Contest than any other country. Riverdance, combining traditional Irish music with innovative Irish dance, has thrilled audiences around the world.

Irish musicians were thrilling Irish audiences for many years before their influence was felt abroad. As one slowly drinks in Irish culture one comes to realise how music and dance are an inseparable part of who the Irish really are.

In May 1999 RTÉ established Lyric FM, Ireland's first full-time classical music station and people who once thought that classical music was only for high brows, are beginning to enjoy the world's great composers. The Irish language radio station, Radio na Gaeltachta, which plays mostly traditional music, has been broadcasting for over thirty years.

Irish identity with language, music and dance intensified in the seventeenth century in resistance to English efforts to strip the Irish of these symbols of national identity. In the late nineteenth and early twentieth centuries as the independence movement began to gain momentum, they represented something that the Irish became determined to take back.

One of the slogans used by the leaders of the Irish independence movement was *Ní tír gan teanga*: a nation without its own language does not exist. In the cultural sense of the term, music and dance were also part of the language. The spoken Irish language and traditional music and dance had deep roots.

Gerald of Wales was closely related to the Norman family of the FitzGeralds, the principal leaders of the Norman invasion of Ireland.[38] A well-educated ecclesiastic, schooled at the University of Paris, Gerald first visited Ireland in 1183 and returned again two years later as part of the entourage of Prince John, Lord of Ireland, son of Henry II. Gerald wrote the first major book ever written about Ireland by a foreign conqueror.[39]

Gerald's views, in their disdain for the Irish, are representative of how most Anglo-Normans viewed the Irish: '... their external characteristics of beard and dress, and internal cultivation of the mind, are so barbarous that they cannot be said to have any culture ... They are a wild and inhospitable people. They live on beasts only, and live like beasts. They have not progressed at all from the primitive habits of pastoral living ... For given only to leisure, and devoted only to laziness, they think the greatest pleasure is not to work, and the greatest wealth is to enjoy liberty ... cut off from well-behaved and law-abiding people, they know only of the barbarous habits in which they were born and brought up, and embrace them as another nature.'

However he also noted: 'It is only in the case of musical instruments that I find any diligence in the people. They seem to me to be incomparably more skilled in these than any other people I have seen.'

This music, concluded Gerald, is 'rounded with the sweetness of charming sonority'. He was entranced by the music he heard in Ireland and amazed by the skill of musicians. What could it be in Irish music that carried this harsh critic of the Irish to realms of such sweetness of charming sonority?

Professor Eugene O'Curry approaches the topic of Ireland's ancient music through a courtship tale involving a Leinster prince, Labhraidh Maen; his tutor, Craftiné, a master harpist who could cast spells through his music; Scoriath, king of west Munster; and his daughter, Moriath.[40] In order to protect his beautiful young daughter from unlawful possession by her suitors, Scoriath required that she be under watch day and night. This prevented any intimate or private conversation between Moriath and any of her possible suitors, including Labhraidh Maen.

The handsome Leinster prince sought assistance from his mentor Craftiné, who advised that the time to speak intimately with the beautiful Moriath would be at a banquet hosted by King Scoriath. The king and his guests had drunk much wine as they listened delightedly to Craftiné perform on his harp. When Craftiné noticed that Labhraidh Maen and Moriath had slipped away from the banquet and were likely out of earshot of his music, he commenced to play the almost magical tones of the *Suantraighé* (pronounced Saun-tree). This sweet music was so soft and enchanting that it threw the whole company, including the king, into a profound slumber.

Craftiné performed the *Suantraighé* until Labhraidh Maen and Moriath returned to their places in the great banqueting hall. During their absence the two had pledged mutual vows of constancy and affection.

According to O'Curry, Craftiné and the other masters of music in ancient Ireland, were obliged by the rules of their order to master, and be perfectly accomplished at, performing three classes or pieces of music. These were the *Suantraighé*, which no one could hear without falling into a deep and delightful slumber; the *Goltraighé* (pronounced Gol-tree), which induced tears and lamentation; and the *Geantraighé* (pronounced Gan-tree), which caused loud and irrepressible laughter.

Craftiné chose to perform a *Geantraighé* as soon as Labhraidh Maen and Moriath had taken their places at the table. The sleeping assembly awakened – unaware that they had dozed off – and began laughing joyously. Craftiné then slipped back into playing ancient beautiful, non-entrancing melodies until the conclusion of the evening's activities. Labhraidh Maen and Moriath were eventually married, and they became king and queen themselves.

P. W. Joyce, another great scholar of early Irish culture, reported on a sense of timelessness brought about by listening to the singing of birds.[41] Common ecclesiastical legends of the Irish medieval era usually involved individual monks becoming entranced by the singing of birds and losing all sense of time. Eventually the bird stops singing, whereupon the monk, thinking that only an hour or two had passed, arises and heads back to the monastery where he notices many strangers and discovers that he had been absent for three hundred years.

Joyce writes that throughout the history of both pagan and Christian Ireland, musicians are always spoken of in the highest of respect: 'Everywhere through the [historical] records we find evidences that the ancient Irish people, both high and low, were passionately fond of music: it entered into their daily life; formed part of their amusements, meetings, and celebrations of every kind.'

The harp is associated with legendary magical feats. These range from the tradition that each harp has a soul or being, to the inherently magic powers of the music which emanated from the plucking of harp strings. Many harpists have called their instrument by name and regarded it as a lover.

The late Derek Bell, former harpist to the Chieftains, wrote that 'the power of [Irish] music was credited with the ability to heal, to cast a spell, to have a very real effect on human life and to invoke the power and support of invisible beings, such as the various nature spirits, angels and gods'.[42] Bell suggested that the 'spiritual hierarchy of our planet chose … [each great western composer] to write very definite forms of music for various aspects of human development'. He stressed that 'music has always been the most occult of all the arts because it "begins where words leave off", and has an absolutely immediate effect on the listener.' He argued that 'We now live in an age where the spiritual hierarchy secretly encourages the spread of the ethnic folk music of all countries ... The higher powers are now inspiring a new interest in ethnic music, art, poetry and folk tales, so that such a universal attitude will be encouraged amongst us all!'

As most music for the harp was composed improvisationally while playing the instrument, or learned by ear, there was no sheet music available for the harp. Several harpists were blind. Having lost their sight due to smallpox, they turned to the harp as the best means to earn a living.

Francis O'Neill wrote about England's attempt to execute harpists, because by their music and songs they were able to stir up animosity toward English rule.[43] A proclamation was issued on 28 January 1603, by the Lord President of Munster, in which the marshal of the province was charged to exterminate all manner of bards and harpists. This was followed by Queen Elizabeth's orders to Lord Barrymore, 'to hang the harpists, wherever found, and destroy their instruments'.

Music was intertwined with both economic and political struggles during significant parts of Irish history. Beginning in the seventeenth century, following their victory at Kinsale, the English tried to 'civilise' the Irish, by forcing them to abandon the Irish language. With the Flight of the Earls in 1607, much of the Irish aristocracy departed for the Continent. As a result many poets and musicians lost their patrons. Thus, in a few decades, harpists who had lived near the top of the native Irish social order for centuries under the patronage of Irish chieftains, began their fall to poverty.

The effect of England's attempt to anglicise the Irish by seeking to prevent its native language and music was double edged. Those who followed the English lead felt ashamed of their native language and music, while those who clove to strong nationalistic tendencies came to see the Irish language and music as symbolising their nature and identity. The former, however, tended to outnumber the latter.

Irrespective of increasingly successful English measures to deprive the Irish of their language and music, there were some who recognised that the creative activity of the harpists which had evolved over several centuries would die without leaving a trace. The first extensive collection of Irish folk music was published in 1726 and featured the tunes of Turlough O'Carolan. Beginning with a meeting of harpists in Granard, County Longford in 1781, and followed by another convocation of harpists in Belfast in 1792, transcribers copied the notes and words of Irish harpists. This effort initiated several attempts to organise a complete notation of many thousand indigenous Irish folk tunes and songs. These tunes came to represent the notated foundation of the explosion of Irish music, aided a century later by the Celtic Revival of the 1890s, which in the twentieth century re-blossomed into a priceless piece of Irish culture heard round the world.

The human voice also carries on the tradition of Irish folk music shaped by the harpists of old. One style of unaccompanied singing is known as *sean-nós* which literally means old style. *Sean-nós* singing can have an emotionally gripping, or almost haunting, effect on the listener. This is due in part to both the structure of the music and the poignant subject matter of the songs themselves.[44]

The subject matter of *sean-nós* singing often suggests suffering from various causes ranging from illness, death, tragedy, exhausting work, loss of a lover, to disappointment in romance. *Sean-nós* songs also dealt with deeply religious themes, occasionally with humour, and sometimes with thinly disguised rebellion and praise for heroes who battled repression.

Ciarán Carson emphasises that the *sean-nós* singer, insofar as traditional Irish music is concerned, seems to act as the medium and transports the audience to the other world. He suggests that this genre represents 'a disembodied medium … appropriate to the *sean-nós* and its lonely desolation. When the singer sings, her vision is turned inward and outward to the interlocking terrain of the song. She may be urged and encouraged by the present circumstances, but she is separate as a singer, and for now, only she knows how to find the pathway to the other world'.[45]

In ancient Ireland, in addition to the harp and timpan (a

stringed instrument played with a bow or plucked with a finger), there were also bagpipes, originally used as war pipes. Pipes were used by the Irish in their War of Independence from the British. I've been told that sometimes the IRA would sound the pipes just seconds before instituting an ambush.

Uilleann pipes were invented in the early eighteenth century because bagpipes had been outlawed by the British. They have a different chanter scale than the bagpipes. Their milder tone is made possible by a softer and more pliable double reed than the shorter, stiffer reed of the bagpipes. The air source for this instrument is a bellows pumped between the left elbow and ribs – rather than by the lungs, as with bagpipes. The musician is normally seated.

There is much phrasal repetition and minimalist shifting in Irish traditional music. There are the slow laments and the faster jigs, reels, and hornpipes. Those latter three terms are also names for dances. Since the sixth-century Irish saint, Columcille, established a monastery in Iona, Irish settlers influenced the development of Scottish culture, including music, dance and the evolution of certain musical instruments. Similarly, the music of the Scots had a significant influence on the development of Irish music.

Irish music has been highly therapeutic due to its transcendental qualities. Music has a spiritual and transporting power that strikes at our very souls. Anyone who is able to be still and receptive can experience the rapture of music and be transported into trance states and encounter other realms of consciousness.

Cork teenager, Ashleigh Ellis, has been composing for the harp since she was seven. When all skilled musicians are performing or composing at their best, something magical happens. 'It's like you don't even know you're really playing. In your mind, you're not thinking about anything. It's as if the music is coming through you. Then you're really doing your best. You know that you won't make a mistake or anything like that. So it's really good. Time just seems to stand still. It just doesn't go anywhere.'

When Ashleigh is composing she hears a tune within her or picks it off on her harp: 'Some things just come to me. Sometimes I'm just fooling around and I hear something I really like, and I stop and write it down. The tune comes from my inner ear. I'm just very still and thinking about music, and all of a sudden I hear a tune in my inner ear.

'Music is unique, it's different than anything else. It's a type of art. It's very like painting because paintings are colours and music is sound and it makes me see pictures.

'When you start learning an instrument and when you do something right it's so thrilling. When you've got it perfect and you can do it absolutely to perfection, that's really good as well, when you can play the whole piece well, it's really nice. You can just play it over and over again.'

Ashleigh's talent as both musician and composer is not surprising considering that both her mother and father are concert violinists. Her mother, Leslie, teaches violin at the Cork School of Music. Her father, Gregory, is the founder and first violinist of Ireland's national string quartet, the Vanbrugh Quartet. Gregory Ellis, of Irish extraction, was raised in England and attended the Royal Academy of Music, London. For the past seventeen years the Vanbrugh Quartet has been a principal source of Ireland's national pride. They has performed all over the world and has over twenty CDs to its credit.

Gregory believes that performing at one's best is a spiritual experience as the music transports both performers and audience into a self-transcending realm where one's most heart-felt feelings are enlivened.

Gregory spends half his day studying scores, rehearsing, or performing in concert. He becomes totally immersed in the sound of his violin and of the instruments of the other three members of the quartet. Their four string instruments bring to life the chamber masterpieces of the world's greatest composers. To bathe oneself in this kind of vibrant sound so many hours a day magnifies the quality of one's life. Gregory reflects this musical influence in a demeanour that is tranquil and subtly joyous.

'When you've got into "the zone", and you are playing at your best, the technicalities no longer become an issue at all. Things start to feel very easy, and when the music is great you start to get very much in tune with the meaning of the music. You feel as though you are being played through – that the music is playing you in a sense. You feel as if you were a boy riding a bicycle. "Look, no hands", as it were. The music is playing itself.

'Music involves emotion as well as the physical aspect of playing it. In performing music you're dealing with different types of emotions; you're having to study these emotions when you are rehearsing. You are trying to get in touch with the emotion that has been left encoded in the musical notes on the page, and when these become a part of yourself you are drawing on your own emotions. You are drawing on your own experiences and there is a sort of synthesis between what the composer is putting down and what is in your background as well.

'I think that when playing at one's best in a string quartet – particularly the works of a great composer – there is a sense that you have joined in some way with the composer, and the composer has brought things out of you that perhaps you didn't even know were there.'

One can infer from Ellis' comments that sometimes the musicians (and perhaps the audience as well) somehow travel to the other world, where the ghost of the long-dead composer whispers to their souls.

When listening to Beethoven's string quartets, especially to the third or middle movement of Opus 132, I often feel as if my soul is lifting itself out of my body and being transported to etheric realms of sublime tranquillity. I feel the presence of a supernatural, soothing energy. A part of me is there in a transcendental realm and another part of me is still in my body listening to the sound of the music.

Ellis explained 'That's Beethoven's Song of Thanksgiving, associated with recovery from an illness. Yes, that movement creates great stillness, and it's as though you are reaching very far down into the depths of your being, to your own ground of being. No matter what troubles have been in the world or in your experience, it's as if you have reached something very comforting and you're building up from that basis, coming from deep down.

'I think that's what's going on as we're playing. It is, as I have noticed afterwards, that when we have been playing at our best that slow, profound music, our breathing calms right down. You lose sense of performing on a platform. You sense the audience is there. And you have a feeling that everyone is sharing the same thing.

'You know how a smell or a scent can suddenly trigger memory. I think it's the same with music. But what's extraordinary about music is that some of those sounds you have never heard before, and yet they still have the power to trigger something. It's just because of the way it's constructed. It's an extraordinary art form. By some kind of intuitive construction and origination of sound, the great composers somehow put across the soul of the music. It's extraordinary how they do it. I think it is one of the greatest achievements of mankind, really – music.

'It is so powerfully transformative that it makes time seem to stand still – in the sense that you are not aware of the past or the future. So in that sense, there is only one time, and that is the present. I think it is fairly clear that when you are totally present in the here and now your sense of time has changed. It can vary between an absolute pinpoint of time to being a vast space in which you have stepped completely out of time.

'Timothy Galway talks about how the unconscious mind is much more subtle and quick and deft. The more you let go of the conscious mind and allow the unconscious mind the freedom to act, the more obviously you're going to have some kind of spontaneous performance. When these moments come, when the entire quartet is playing at its best, there is a radiance in the music, and ecstasy. It is very much like intoxication, in a sense that nothing can go wrong.

'But being aware of yourself in that flow is almost a scary thought. Because if you are thinking that thought, you are not in the here and now. So that, itself, is a danger. It's something which you catch out of the corner of your eye. It's not something that you look at straight in the face.'

At the West Cork Chamber Music Festival in Bantry I heard Martin Hayes, the fiddler, play live for the first time. Nearly all the classical string musicians at the festival, from all over the world, were in the audience to hear him perform. Martin, and Denis Cahill on guitar, transported the audience into some far away part of the galaxy and they were called back for one encore after another. It seemed that in each successive encore they carried the audience with them deeper and deeper into the realms of musical bliss.

The audience was on its feet with applause, led by the string players with tears flowing down their cheeks. Gregory Ellis and

I went backstage to congratulate Martin. Gregory told Martin 'Yours was one of the most profoundly spectacular performances I've ever heard in my entire life.'

Later Martin Hayes said that performing at his very best was 'the most contented I'll ever be. You can't be thinking about it while it's happening. So it's the kind of experience you look back to afterwards. There wouldn't be a whole lot of thoughts going on and yet you would be precisely aware of everything. It's very much about being completely in the moment. It's as if your body were playing the music, you know – you burst into playing the music and you didn't have self-thoughts. During the performance you're trying to work your way out of self-conscious thoughts, so you work your way into the moment where the piece of music and yourself are not something that you could distinguish apart.

'Playing music parallels what you would read about in various world spiritualities and religions of that ultimate experience. They talk about life in totality and the way you live your life when they talk in those spiritual terms. But I find that I can have that experience in music.

'Many composers and musicians attribute their music to a source outside themselves, like an encounter with fairies and spirits late at night in a field. A person may feel inspired and not know where to attribute the source. I think the singular claiming of authorship in the arts can be a big blockage and mistake. You have to be able to pass on the acclaim to another source.'

Martin Hayes is very knowledgeable about the mystical dimensions of the musical experience. Listening to him describe musically-induced altered states of consciousness reminded me of the writings of the mystics St John of the Cross and Meister Eckhard.

Eckehard Krupp was born and raised in Germany. He became so entranced by Irish music that he came to Ireland to perform with traditional musicians. Eckehard married an Irish woman. Eckie, as he is known on Ireland's Beara peninsula, performs on flute, banjo and guitar. He is also teaching himself the fiddle.

What the mystical Eckhard had in common with the musical Eckehard is that they both frequently experienced unitive states. 'The moment I enter that state there is no time involved.

Time stands still. You go beyond your personal being. You leave your body and the limits of your body as your body itself is limited by time. It is like I have gone from birth to death, and at that intensely feeling plane when I am at the higher level – the spirit level – I get out of my body and experience timelessness, just as a medium who leaves the body. You let yourself out into the room and you don't any longer need a visual stimulus … You close your eyes and the music fills everything. It's a perfect kind of situation when you have abandoned any need for time. Afterwards I often feel a deep thankfulness for the experience.

'It is the spirit part of me that has the experience. My own spirit, through music, goes into a religious state. During this transcendental experience with a higher being – call it God or nature – I am carried there by the music. Music is a constant companionship to me. It gives me a security in my life.'

The soprano, Noirín Ní Riain, a well-known Irish *sean-nós* singer, who also often sings with musical accompaniment, takes this a notch closer to actual Divine presence. Paralleling the theological concept of theophany – the appearance of God – when her singing is most spiritual she feels that a 'theosony' – the sound of God – occurs. Instead of appearing in an apparition, God appears in sound. She becomes an instrument for the Divine. Noirín is convinced that when she is performing at her best the energy moving her vocal chords is Divine energy.

'Theosony is a word I made up myself. It is a mixture of theology and sonance. I realised on an intuitive level that there was an actual sound of God and that a particular song could actually give you the sound of God.

'The deepest singing for me would probably be when I'm on my own. I don't think it happens when I'm before an audience. It has always happened before the event. I look to the Holy Spirit to present me with what I am supposed to do next in singing. I have the patience to wait for guidance on what I am to sing next out of my repertoire.

'Things happen. It's like being touched by a ghost. When I sing Hildegard of Bingen, I am very comfortable working with her spirit and conscious of her power over me at that particular moment. If it is for the transformation of others the music just works and everything seems to fall into place.

'The Hildegard *Kyrie* is an extraordinary piece of music. I don't know where it comes from. It's just the most inspired piece of music I ever heard. It is a very powerful experience for me.

'Another was when I was in Kosovo singing in the barracks to refugees. I was improvising and something came through me that must have been pre-Christian, that was extraordinary. I just couldn't get it out of my system. I felt the power of music just lift them for one moment out of what they were suffering. It was a tranformative religious experience. It was a theosony that had nothing to do with me. It was just something that came through me. It's extraordinary – the power of music and how you have no control over it.'

Virginia Kerr, a renowned Irish soprano, also feels that when she is 'singing at my best – in addition to losing sense of time – an energy comes through my vocal chords that gives them a greater freedom, quality and power. I feel totally free of any tension, which gives me the ability to let them do their job and therefore reach their full potential. Because I would be totally relaxed, I am able to allow this positive energy to flow through.'

Gerry Kelly is a fine cellist who teaches at the Cork School of Music. He also experiences 'the suspension of time'. He acquires the power to play his instrument more masterfully and to communicate more intimately with his audience. 'They pick up on whatever kind of waves I send out and what they send back to me enhances our communications still further.'

Communication with his audience is particularly heightened when he is playing at his best at special concerts for children. 'If the music is good and it's being played well, they respond very attentively to what you are doing. My own reaction to their response is deeply emotional. I am very moved because their reaction is so pure and they are totally committed to the music. I feel that the children can pull me in with them. When that happens you know that's why you live to play music and you wish every performance was like that.'

Gerry has done many special concerts for children, and sometimes he wears a gorilla suit. It seems to cause more excitement for the kids, as they suspect that no gorilla knows how to play a cello. It's not easy to get children to sit still for classical music. 'Kids either love it or hate it.' He feels the minds of children are so clear that they don't have a predetermined agenda. They tune in or they don't.

'When they are tuned in, it is so moving because they are getting the message of the music. When I'm playing with my gorilla suit on, sometimes I can feel the tears rolling down my cheeks and dripping onto the inside of the mask. You just know that they are picking up on this music for what it really is, that they pick up on the value of the music and resonate with it at a very deep level. They mightn't be able to put that into words in any way, but you know they are connected with you and the music from the intensity of their attentiveness.'

Gerry believes that a good musician must do more than play his instrument well. He must be able to communicate to the audience the message of the music. He likes to tell a story about Billy Dunwoody who years ago taught the flute in Belfast to the now-renowned James Galway. Dunwoody said that each great musician is able to convey a profound musical message because he 'has the message'. Occasionally a musician would ask him, 'Do I have the message?' Dunwoody would answer, 'If you have to ask me …'

'There is some great force that comes through you when you're playing at your best. You can't push it. You have to try and get into a state of acceptance. It's like a Zen thing. If you are trying too hard to hit the target, you'll miss it. It's like becoming one with the target so that you allow yourself to become the target. You have to let go of all thoughts and allow the music to come through you.'

Mary Nunan, a dancer and choreographer, is on the faculty of the University of Limerick. Her tradition within contemporary or modern dance pertains to the exploration of movement. For Mary, the creative act of choreography is like taking a journey. 'Forms or styles emerge, but always through the development of your personal style, and by exploring how you want to use movement in order to express what you want to communicate as an artist. But the most important aspect of being a choreographer is the journey. This sometimes involves interactions with the dancers who participate in the creation. This dialogue is part of the journey.

'You need to have the ability to be absolutely open to surprises. I tend to plan out the progressions, but then something happens and the piece itself starts speaking to you. It takes on a life of its own. You end up negotiating with the piece as well as

with your own ideas and the dancers. You get a better understanding of your own idea by letting it go and watching it express itself in movement. Its dimensions then reveal themselves
to you. That way you can usually end up with both feeling-
intention and structure, or form integrated and in harmony, so
the whole thing really works.'

There seemed to be an echo in what Mary said of what musicians reported about performing at their best: the music sometimes seems to play them, rather than their playing the music.

'You discover things. You discover depths in the material
you never expected to encounter or realised were there. It's amaz-
ing how much you discover about the piece. You are totally
engaged with it with such freshness it feels like you're doing it
for the first time. You become one with it. You're there and it is
revealing itself to you. And you get right into the action of the
piece and you're doing it so well you feel, "That's it!"'

All these performers share a common capacity for tuning into
some other dimension of consciousness, while expressing their
art form. Part of them is completely tuned in to the music or the
dance, while another part has opened up, or surrendered, to
some external influence or energy that courses through their
consciousness, filling them with inspiration and creativity. It is
as if they are transported to, and suspended within, the aesth-
etic-spiritual interface. Often, when this mystical moment occurs,
they experience going beyond time.

Ciarán Carson commented on the mystical essence of music:
'being in tune is a function of time. You are in tune with what
goes on. It is the way the players become blue votaries of time,
and intercede with it, and beat their time in slightly different
times embedded in their pedal movements. One rocks off his
heel on the off-beat; another taps the noiseless air one inch above
the floor; another dances, almost with two feet. Many very good
players don't budge their feet at all. They are moving to an inner
pulse.

'Time accelerates or contracts. We make a contract with it to
pretend that it will never overcome us. The space of the song is
what – how many minutes? – but seven years have gone by and
we are still waiting for a resolution.'[46]

What is it about the power of music in Ireland? How is it

that the Irish seem to be born with an ear for music and allow it to fill their souls? The Irish conversational voice is nearly as musical as an Irish air performed by an ancient harpist or a group of traditional musicians. How are the Irish so sensitive to the power of sound, so able and willing to let it transport them to other realms?

According to Micheál Ó Súilleabháin, a contemporary Irish composer: 'How you dance is how you hold yourself, how you speak is how you sound, and how you sound is so intimate with yourself … What I am essentially doing is arguing for the realisation of the power of the arts – and of music and dance in this instance – as a force within our lives … "the transgressive element of music" as a special power which it can have in re-shaping society. Music here is like air – there is a sense in which it is not easily controlled. Even if you shut all the cultural doors, it can still come in under them.

'This extraordinary island, so much alive and vibrant with the arts, so local in its groundedness and so international in its search, continues to increasingly astound those who view us from without, even as more and more of us who are players on the ground grow into a realisation of the artistic riches which surround us.'[47]

If Gerald of Wales observed the musical culture of present day Ireland, he almost certainly would reaffirm his original judgement about Ireland's musical genius and also conclude that it is still very much alive.

KERNELS OF IRISHNESS

It was over sixty years ago when my grandfather started telling me stories about Ireland that he himself had heard as a young lad sitting on his Irish grandmother's knee. Some of these stories contained local legend. When I visit Bandon, the hometown of my Irish ancestors, I can occasionally still hear some of the same legends being repeated there. Over a hundred and fifty years have passed since my grandfather's grandmother boarded a sailing vessel to flee Ireland's famine by crossing the Atlantic Ocean and making a new home in America.

There have been many changes in Ireland since then. Ireland is no longer a British colony. Irish Protestants presently constitute less than five per cent of the population and they no longer control the Irish economy. Far fewer Irish speak Irish, and everyone can speak English.

The changes between Ireland of a century and a half ago and the present day are so numerous that it would take several thick tomes to document the differences. Even in the thirty years that have passed since I first set foot on Irish soil, the changes have been enormous. Farmers don't haul their milk to the creamery aboard donkey carts, nor plough their fields with horses. Now they tow their milk in large stainless steel canisters or the cream-ery sends its trucks to their farm to collect the milk. They plough their fields with tractors.

Thirty years ago most of the adult population transported themselves on foot or bicycles. Now nearly every family has more than one car.

Three decades ago some of the richest men in rural Ireland wore collarless grandfather shirts and woollen tweed jackets covered with many patches and wore gabardine trousers stuffed into rubber Wellington boots known as 'wellies', just like the poor man dressed. Now, many of the rural affluent cruise around in designer clothes, driving their new Mercedes or Volvo.

My guess would be that thirty years ago the average age of nuns would have been forty while today the average age would be more like seventy-five, with far fewer of them.

Thirty years ago the economy of Ireland was so depressed that finding a job often required emigrating to another country. For nearly a decade Ireland's Gross National Product has ex-panded at an unprecedented annual rate. Thirty years ago Ire-land was regarded economically as a third world country. Now it is referred to as the Celtic Tiger.

Nearly every middle-aged or older Irish person will agree that much has changed and quickly point to dozens of differ-ences between the Ireland of their youth and that of the present day.

Through watching American and British movies portraying the glories of a materialistic culture, and by being bombarded with advertising, a growing number of Irish are beginning to be-lieve that they are what they buy. They are learning to measure their self-worth by the clothes they wear, the houses they live in and the cars they drive. The more they have, the better they tend to feel about themselves.

This trend seems to have affected the big-spender, under-thirty-five generation, more drastically than it has the over fifty. The older generation too is spending more, but also holds the memory of hardship in Ireland. This consciousness tempers spending urges among the post-middle-aged as some fear of re-current poverty remains alive. The thirty-five to fifty generation appears to vacillate between big spending and sensible saving.

Acquisitiveness, as the leading component of the new value

system, affects most age brackets in Ireland. In fact, increasing numbers of Irish – both rural and urban – believe that they are losing their Irishness because of it. Many fear 'we're nearly no different now than Yanks or Brits'.

Their mistake is in assuming that their belongings are the principal means of demonstrating their collective identity. Many appear to forget that social and cultural identity are shaped by more than material possessions alone.

When they drive by archaeological ruins, they may unconsciously assume that there is no relationship between the people who built those structures and themselves. This attitude reflects a belief that what is past has no value and that there are no ancestral links between themselves and the builders of those ancient architectural creations.

Yet, when they fly back to Ireland from a visit abroad and look down at the rural landscape and see green fields bordered by ancient stone boundary walls, their hearts tell them that they have come home.

The certain traits that exist and are readily observable among the Irish are the starting point of this book. I have sought to examine by observation and reflection upon my experiences with Irish friends – aided by some reading and historical research – what it is like to be Irish, particularly in a rural setting. Although I have visited virtually every county within the Republic of Ireland, most of my opportunities to observe and engage with the Irish have occurred in predominantly rural South Kerry and West Cork. These are the areas where I spend most of my time when I visit Ireland.

Much of what I have concluded about the Irish generally, and the rural Irish specifically, is based upon direct observational experience. Also, much of what I have concluded is generally positive. There is, however, a dark side to the Irish which J. P. Donleavy captured in part with slagging humour in his book, *A Singular Country*. There is a long line of authors, starting with Gerald of Wales, Edmund Spenser, and others – most of whom were English – who have castigated the Irish.[48] As a result of such writings or other beratements over the past twelve centuries inflicted upon the Irish by invading conqueror-settlers, the Irish were taught that to gain the respect of their conquerors, they should abandon what is Irish about them and conform to other models of language, laws, value systems and behaviour.

Though the Irish largely succeeded in converting the Vikings and the Normans to using the Irish language and to adopting Irish customs and values, the English succeeded in beating the Irish down into adopting their language, laws and social systems, even though it took them nearly half a millennium to do so.

Nevertheless, the Irish resistance to conform to the English persisted, and they won the War of Independence against the British. The Irish, however, paid a huge economic price for their independence. This entailed paying highly inflated amounts for imported English goods and being subjected to high duties for Irish goods exported to England, plus losses of certain traditional English markets for Irish goods. Also involved in the creation of an independent Irish state was the need to rebuild the economy, in addition to first subjecting itself to a debilitating civil war.

My sense of what it means to be Irish is revealed by this history, and by words, attitudes, behaviours and values. Combinations of these qualities occur abundantly in Ireland, and have done so for many centuries, though certainly not in equal measure in every Irish person. But there is a prevalence of such indicators which I have observed that do suggest what it means to be Irish. The pursuit of identifying such indicators has been, over the past thirty years, a true adventure into discovering the contents of the Irish heart and soul which I like to refer to as the Emerald spirit.

When I discussed what I consider to be individual Irish traits with Irish friends, I have sometimes encountered disbelieving reactions: 'What is so uniquely Irish about that trait? Other people from elsewhere behave the same way.' Undoubtedly they do. But it is the combination of these various factors, along with the land, climate and cultural tradition in which the person dwells, that renders the person Irish.

In each of the previous chapters I have identified and discussed a number of distinct kernels of Irishness. I have explored the Irish approach to the intricacies of the weather, vicissitudes of nature, power of place and sense of community, honouring of the dead and appreciation of the privilege of being alive, seeing some good in every person, conversation as a means of intimate connection, consciousness of, and connectedness to, the other world and its diversity of population – from banshee to Blessed Virgin Mother – and finally, the transcendental pleasures of music and dance. These are the kernels. But what is the whole, or is there a whole? Are there at least common threads?

I sense there are unifying elements. I believe that there is much more to the Irish than the sum of the parts. They often exhibit an acute sensitivity toward whatever is going on around them. They notice with great intensity what their senses are showing them. They perceive patterns and nuances with quick-wittedness and heightened awareness. When what they are perceiving becomes familiar to them, they often tend to form a connection with it. Sometimes they identify with it, as if making it a part of who they are, or at least recognising it as a welcome part of their environment. The 'I' and the 'you' become an 'us'. The 'I' and the 'place', or 'environmental phenomenon', become an extension of each other.

This communion takes place almost unnoticed among the Irish, and at a very deep level. It occurs, I believe, in the heart and soul. When they live out of their heart and soul, it shows. They exude a reverence for being alive, humility, kindness, compassion, graciousness, sociability, cheerfulness, and humour. They live largely in the present moment, vibrantly. They understand, breathe and manifest what so many others can only imagine and hope for. For most of the Irish, life is much more fun than grief.

From the ancient roots of these traits, habits, characteristics, values and behaviours I sense that so many Irish people continue to immensely enjoy the excitement of plunging into each new day. They thrive at a dimension in which the tangible and intangible are somehow intertwined. This state of being appears to produce for them a remarkable quality of life.

I have done the best I can at grasping the Irish essence. I'm going to stop now because, I know deep down inside myself that the brilliant travel writer, H. V. Morton, was right: 'Any book on Ireland must be full of contradictions and thoughts that may be only half true'.

FOOTNOTES

See bibliography for full citations

1 The legend of the stone of Fal and Conn is contained in an ancient Irish manuscript (Harleian, 5280) housed in the British Museum

2 Frank Mitchell and Michael Ryan, *Reading the Irish Landscape*

3 *Glanerought and the Petty Fitzmaurices*

4 The 10 per cent tax dating from the 1820s on the value of annual produce from lands, used to support the local Protestant Clergyman – a tax not favoured by the predominantly Catholic tenants

5 For a scholarly and quite readable discourse on this topic, *see* Mary Low's *Celtic Christianity and Nature*

6 Joyce, P. W., *A Social History of Ancient Ireland*

7 As quoted in Standish H. O'Grady's *Silva Gadelica*

8 Kelly, Fergus, *A Guide to Early Irish Law*

9 MacCana, Proinsias, 'Notes on the Early Irish Concept of Unity'

10 Heaney, Seamus, *The Government of the Tongue*

11 Kelly, Fergus *A Guide to Early Irish Law*

12 Gerald of Wales, *The History and Topography of Ireland*

13 Hughes, Kathleen, *Early Christian Ireland*

14 Yeats, W. B., *Essays and Introductions*

15 Rees, Alwyn & Brinley, *Celtic Heritage*

16 Carey, John, *A Single Ray of the Sun*

17 Bonwick, James, *Irish Druids and Old Irish Religions*

18 Green, Miranda J., *The Celtic World*

19 Joyce, P. W., *A Social History of Ancient Ireland*

20 O'Rahilly, Thomas F., *Early Irish History and Mythology*

21 Keating, Geoffrey, *History of Ireland, see* P. W. Joyce for citation

22 Carey, John, *A Single Ray of the Sun*

23 *The Book of Druimm*, an eighth-century manuscript, lost in the seventeenth century; also cited as *Cín Dromma Snechtaí, see* Carey, John 'On the Interrelationships of some Cín Dromma Snechtaí texts', *Eriu* 46 (1995), pp. 71-92

24 Patch, Howard, *The Other World*

25 Plummer, Charles, 'Bethada Naem n Erenn' in *Lives of Irish Saints*

26 Plummer, Charles, 'Life of St Coemgen' in *Lives of Irish Saints*

27 Ross, Anne, 'Ritual and the Druids'

28 Carey, John, 'Native Elements in Irish Pseudohistory'

29 *Lebor Gabala*: *The Book of Invasions*

30 Moriarty, John, *Dreamtime*

31 Lysaght, Patricia, *The Banshee*

32 John Dunne's book, *Haunted Ireland*, is filled with accounts of such ghostly activities

33 For other accounts of poltergeist (from the German term meaning 'noisy ghost') experiences, *see* Alexander Imich, Incredible Tales of the Paranormal, Bramble Books, New York, 1995

34 Yeats, W. B., *Autobiography*

35 MacManus, Dermot, 'Hostile Spirits and Hurtful Spells' in *The Middle Kingdom*

36 An interesting and well-organised source for further information on this topic is Peter Harbison's *Pilgrimages in Ireland*

37 James, William, *Varieties of Religious Experience*

38 Otherwise known as Giraldus de Barri, or Giraldus Cambrensis – from Cambria, the Latin name for Wales

39 *The History and Topography of Ireland*

40 O'Curry, Eugene, *Lectures on the Manuscript Materials of Ancient Irish History*

41 Joyce, P. W., *A Social History of Ancient Ireland*, vol. I

42 Bell's preface to Walton, Russell, *A Harp of Fishbones*

43 O'Neill, Francis, *Irish Minstrels and Musicians*

44 Ó Canainn, Tomás, *Traditional Music in Ireland*

45 Carson, Ciarán, *Last Night's Fun*

46 Carson, Ciarán, *Last Night's Fun*

47 Ó Súilleabháin, Micheál, in Pine, Richard (ed.), *Music in Ireland 1848-1998*

48 Spenser, Edmund, *A View of the Present State of Ireland*

BIBLIOGRAPHY

Æ (Russell, George), *The Candle of Vision*, Macmillan and Co., London, 1918

Apolito, Paolo, *Apparitions of the Madonna at Oliveto Citra*, translated by William A. Christian, Jr, tr., The Pennsylvania State University Press, University Park, 1998

Bainton, Roland H., *Christianity*, Houghton & Mifflin, Boston, 1964

Bonwick, James, *Irish Druids and Old Irish Religions*, Dorset Press, New York, 1986

Brennan, Helen, *The Story of Irish Dance*, Brandon, Dingle, 1999

Byrne, Donn, *Ireland: The Rock Whence I Was Hewn*, Sampson Low, Marsten, London, 1928

Cabot, David, *Irish Birds*, Harper Collins, London, 1995

Carey, John, *A Single Ray of the Sun*, Celtic Studies Publications, Andover, 1999

Carey, John, 'Native Elements in Irish Pseudohistory' in Doris Edel, ed., *Cultural Identity and Cultural Integration*, Blackrock, Dublin 1995

Carmichael, Alexander, *Carmina Gadelica*, Edinburgh, 1928

Carney, James, *Studies in Irish Literature and History*, Dublin Institute For Advanced Studies, Dublin, 1979

Carson, Ciaran, *Last Night's Fun*, Pimliko, London, 1996

Chaboud, René, *Weather: Drama of the Heavens*, Discoveries/Harry N. Abrams, N.Y., 1996

Chadwick, Nora, *The Celts*, Penguin, Middlesex, 1970

Connolly, S. J., *The Oxford Companion to Irish History*, Oxford University Press, Oxford, 1998

Corish, Patrick, *The Irish Catholic Experience: A Historical Survey*, Gill and Macmillian, Dublin, 1985

Craig, Patricia, *The Oxford Book of Ireland*, Oxford University Press, Oxford, 1998

Cullen, Louis, *The Hidden Ireland: Reassessment of a Concept*, Lilliput Press, Dublin, 1998

Cuppage, Judith, *Archaeological Survey of the Dingle Peninsula*, Oidhreacht Chorca Dhuibhne, Ballyferriter, 1986

D'Arcy, Gordon, *The Birds Of Ireland*, Appletree Press, Belfast, 1986

Dobyns, Stephen, *Common Carnage*, Penguin Poets, New York, 1996

Dolan, Terence Patrick, *A Dictionary of Hiberno-English*, Gill and Macmillan, Dublin, 1998

Donleavy, J. P., *A Singular Country*, W. W. Norton & Co., New York, 1990

Dunne, John J., *Haunted Ireland*, Appletree Press, Belfast, 1977, 1984

Feehan, John M., *My Village, My World*, Mercier Press, Cork, 1991

Flynn, Arthur, *Irish Dance*, Appletree Press, Belfast, 1998

Gantz, Jeffrey, *Early Irish Myths and Sagas*, Penguin Books, London, 1981

Gerald of Wales, *The History and Topography of Ireland*, John J. O'Meara, tr., Penguin Books, Middlesex, 1982

Gray, Elizabeth A., tr., *Cathmaige Tuired: The Second Battle of Mag Tuired*, Irish Texts Society, London, 1982

Green, Miranda, ed., *The Celtic World*, Routledge Press, London, 1995

Green, Miranda, ed., *Celtic Myths*, British Museum Press, London, 1993

Greene, David & O'Connor, Frank, *A Golden Treasury of Irish Poetry: AD 600–1200*, Brandon, Dingle, 1990

Gregory, Lady, *Complete Irish Mythology*, Stanley Press, London, 1994; originally published in separate volumes as: *Gods and Fighting Men*, 1904, and *Cúchulainn of Muirthemme*, 1902, by John Murray Publishers, London

Hanson, R. P. C., *The Life and Writings of the Historical Saint Patrick*, Seabury Press, New York, 1983

Hanson, R. P. C., *Saint Patrick: His Origins and Career*, Oxford University Press, Oxford, 1968

Harbison, Peter, *Pilgrimages in Ireland*, Barrie & Jenkins, London, 1991

Hardy, Ralph, *Weather: Drama of the Heavens*, Harry N. Abrams (Discoveries series), New York, 1996

Heaney, Seamus, *The Spirit Level*, Faber and Faber, London, 1996

Heaney, Seamus, *Seeing Things*, Faber and Faber, London, 1991

Heaney, Seamus, *The Government of the Tongue*, Faber and Faber, London, 1988

Heaney, Seamus, *New Selected Poems 1966–1987*, Faber and Faber, London, 1988

Heaney, Seamus, *Sweeney Astray*, Faber and Faber, London, 1983

Heaney, Seamus, *Selected Poems 1965–75*, Faber and Faber, London, 1976

Herm, Gerhard, *The Celts*, St Martin's Press, New York, 1975

Hickey, Donal, *Stone Mad For Music; The Sliabh Luachra Story*, Marino Books, Dublin, 1999

Hoagland, Kathleen, ed., *1000 Years of Irish Poetry*, Konecky & Konecky, New York, 1974

Hubert, Henri, *The Greatness and Decline of the Celts*, Constable, London, 1934

Hughes, Kathleen, *Early Christian Ireland*, Cornell University Press, Ithaca, 1972

Ignatius of Loyola, *The Spiritual Exercises of St Ignatius*, Anthony Mottola, tr., Image Books, Garden City, 1964

Imich, Alexander, *Incredible Tales of the Paranormal*, Bramble Books, New York, 1995

James, William, *The Varieties of Religious Experience: A Study In Human Nature*, Edinburgh, 1902

Joyce, P. W., *A Social History of Ancient Ireland*, M. H. Gill and Son, Dublin, 1920 tr., *Keating's History of Ireland (Forus Feasa ar Erinn)*; also translated by Comyn, David, for the Irish Texts Society, Dublin, 1938; also translated by Dineen, Patrick S., for the Irish Text Society, 1914; additionally translated by O'Mahony, John, as cited in Joyce, P. W., *A Social History of Ancient Ireland, supra.*

Kahl, Jonathan D. W., *National Audubon Society, First Field Guide: Weather,* Scholastic, New York, 1998

Kavanagh, Patrick, *The Green Fool,* Penguin Books, London, 1938, 1971

Keane, John B., *A Warm Bed on a Cold Night,* Mercier Press, Cork, 1997

Kelly, Fergus, *A Guide to Early Irish Law,* Dublin Institute for Advanced Studies, Dublin, 1988

Kelly, J. N. D., *Early Christian Creeds,* Longman, New York, 1972

Kenney, James T., *The Sources of the Early History of Ireland: Ecclesiastical,* Padraig Ó Taillinir, Dublin, 1929

Kenny, Mary, *Goodbye to Catholic Ireland,* Sinclair-Stevenson, London, 1997

Kinsella, Thomas, *The New Oxford Book of Irish Verse,* Oxford University Press, Oxford, 1986

Lenihan, Edmund, *In Search of Biddy Early,* Mercier Press, Cork, 1987

Llywelyn, Morgan, *The Essential Library for Irish Americans,* Tom Doherty Associates, New York, 1999

Low, Mary, *Celtic Christianity and Nature,* Edinburgh University Press, Edinburgh, 1996

Lysaght, Patricia, *The Banshee,* Glendale Press, 1986, and O'Brien Press, Dublin, 1996

Maher, Michael, ed., *Irish Spirituality,* Veritas, Dublin, 1981

McCrum, Robert; Cran, William; & MacNeil, Robert, *The Study of English,* Viking, New York, 1986

McManus, Dermot, *The Middle Kingdom,* Colin Smythe Limited., Buckinghamshire, 1973

McWilliams, Brendan, *A Weather Eye on Literature,* Irish Times books, Dublin, 1996

Meyer, Kuno, *Ancient Irish Poetry,* Constable and Company, London, 1913, 1994

Mitchell, Frank, & Ryan, Michael, *Reading the Irish Landscape,* Town House, Dublin, 1998

Moriarty, John, *Nostos,* Lilliput Press, Dublin, 2001

Moriarty, John, *Dreamtime,* Lilliput Press, Dublin, 1994, 1999

Morton, H. V., *In Search of Ireland,* Methuen, London, 1930, 1984

Muldoon, Paul, ed., *The Faber Book of Contemporary Irish Poetry,* Faber and Faber, London, 1986

Murphy, Gerard, *Early Irish Lyrics,* Four Courts Press, Dublin, 1956, 1998

O'Brien, Jacqueline, & Harbison, Peter, *Ancient Ireland,* Weidenfeld and Nicholson, London, 1996

Ó Corráin, Donnchadh; Breatnach, Liam; & McCone, Kim, eds., *Sages, Saints and Storytellers*, An Sagart, Maynooth, 1989

O'Curry, Eugene, *Lectures on the Manuscript Materials of Ancient Irish History*, Four Courts Press, Dublin, 1861, 1995

Ó Duinn, Seán, *Where Three Streams Meet: Celtic Spirituality*, The Columba Press, Dublin, 2000

O'Grady, Standish H., *Silva Gadelica*, Williams and Norgate, London, 1892

Ó hÓgain, Dáithí, *The Sacred Isle: Belief and Religion in Pre-Christian Ireland*, Collins Press, Wilton, Cork 1999

O'Leary, Con, *A Wayfarer In Ireland*, Methuen, London, 1935

Ó Luanaigh, Tomás B., *An Chainnt Bhrea V*, Tuosist Parish Press, Lauragh, 2002

Ó Muirithe, Diarmuid, *A Dictionary of Anglo-Irish*, Four Courts Press, Dublin, 1996

O'Neill, Francis, *Irish Minstrels and Musicians*, Mercier Press, Cork, 1913, 1987

O'Rahilly, Thomas, F., *Early Irish History and Mythology*, Dublin Institute for Advanced Studies, Dublin, 1976

Ó Suilleabháin, Seán, *Irish Wake Amusements*, Mercier Press, Cork, 1967, 1997

Ó Tuama, Seán, & Kinsella, Thomas, *An Duanaire; 1600–1900: Poems of the Dispossessed*, Dolmen Press, Dublin, 1981

Patch, Howard Rollin, *The Other World*, Harvard University Press, Cambridge, 1950

Pierce, David, *Yeats' Worlds*, Yale University Press, New Haven, 1995

Piggott, Stuart, *The Druids*, Thames and Hudson, London, 1968

Pine, Richard, ed., *Music in Ireland 1848–1998*, Mercier Press, Cork, 1998

Plummer, Charles, *Lives of Irish Saints*, Oxford University Press, London, 1922

Powell, I. G. E., *The Celts*, Thames and Hudson, London, 1980

Raftery, Joseph, *The Celts*, Mercier Press, Cork, 1964

Rees, Alywn and Brinley, *Celtic Heritage*, Thames and Hudson, London, 1961, 1990

Riordan, John D., *Irish Catholics: Tradition and Transitions*, Veritas, Dublin, 1980

Ross, Anne, 'Ritual and the Druids', chapter 23 in Miranda Green's *The Celtic World*, Routledge Press, London, 1995

Ryan, Tim, & Kirakowski, Jurek, *Ballinspittle: Moving Statues and Faith*, Mercier Press, Cork, 1985

Shaw, George Bernard, *John Bull's Other Ireland*, London, 1926

Somerset Fry, Peter & Fiona, *A History of Ireland*, Barnes and Noble, New York, 1988, 1993

Spenser, Edmond, *A View of the Present State of Ireland*, ed. by Renwick,

W.L., Doubleday, New York, 1970

Titley, Alan, *A Pocket History of Gaelic Culture*, O'Brien Press, Dublin, 2000

Walker, Dorothy, *Louis le Brocquy*, Ward River Press, Dublin, 1981

Wallace, Martin, *A Short History of Ireland*, Appletree Press, Belfast, 1973, 1986

Walton, Russell, *A Harp of Fishbones*, White Row Press, Belfast, 1992

Wand, J. W. C., *A History of the Early Church to AD500*, Methuen, London, 1937

Waters, John, *An Intelligent Person's Guide to Modern Ireland*, Duckworth, London, 1997

Wentz, W. Y. Evans, *The Fairy-Faith In Celtic Countries*, Oxford University Press, Oxford, 1911; Colin Smythe Limited, Buckinghamshire, 1977

Yeats, W. B., *Selected Poetry*, A. Norman Jeffers, ed., Macmillan, London, 1962

Yeats, W. B., *Essays and Introductions*, Macmillan, New York, 1961;

Yeats, W. B., *Autobiography*, Gill and Macmillan, London, 1955